Afterplay

Afterplay

A KEY TO INTIMACY

James Halpern, Ph.D. and
Mark A. Sherman, Ph.D.

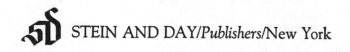

STEIN AND DAY/*Publishers*/New York

First published in 1979
Copyright © 1979 by James Halpern and Mark A. Sherman
All rights reserved
Designed by Ed Kaplin
Printed in the United States of America
Stein and Day/*Publishers*/Scarborough House,
Briarcliff Manor, N.Y. 10510

Library of Congress Cataloging in Publication Data

Halpern, James,

    Afterplay.

    Bibliography: p. 202
    Includes index.
    1. Orgasm.   2. Sex customs—United States.
3. Sex—Psychology.   I. Sherman, Mark, joint author.   II. Title.
HQ31.S622   301.41'8   79-679
ISBN 0-8128-2572-1

*To our mothers
and the memory of
our fathers*

ACKNOWLEDGMENTS

We gratefully acknowledge the help of the men and women who distributed the questionnaires and all those people who took the time to complete them. We thank them for teaching something to all of us.

We would like to thank our research assistant, Kathryn Isaacs, whose intelligence, enthusiasm, and just plain hard work were indispensable. Likewise for the two people who typed the manuscript, Marie Girard and Susan Davison. In addition to their impeccable typing, they showed at least as much knowledge of the English language as did the authors. Renni Brown did a superb job carefully editing the entire manuscript. A number of other people also made helpful suggestions: Joyce Frommer, Sheri Safran, Dr. Richard Sloan, Sol Stein, Marilee Talman, Robert B. Taylor, M.D., and Paul Toro.

This book benefited greatly from the substantive contributions of our wives, Shelley Sherman and Ilsa Halpern. We also thank them and the other members of our families—Jonathan and Eric Sherman, and Nathan and Willow Halpern—for their love and support.

Grateful acknowledgment is made to the following for permission to reprint excerpts from published materials:

Alfred A. Knopf, Inc.: *Combat in the Erogenous Zone* by Ingrid Bengis, © 1972 by Ingrid Bengis.

Judith Coburn: "Orgasm: Pleasure or Tyranny?" which appeared in *Mademoiselle*, May 1978, © 1978 by The Condé Nast Publications, Inc.

Random House, Inc.: *Final Payments* by Mary Gordon, © 1978 by Mary Gordon.

Macmillan Publishing Co., Inc.: *The Hite Report* by Shere Hite, © 1976 by Shere Hite.

Institute for Sex Research: *Sexual Behavior in the Human Female* by A. Kinsey, W. Pomeroy, C. Martin, and P. H. Gebhard, © by Paul H. Gebhard. Original copyright, 1953 by W. B. Saunders Co.

CONTENTS

CHAPTER 1

What Is Afterplay?

It has been more than two years since we first discussed the idea that became this book. Actually, in the very beginning we did not even have a word for what we were talking about. But we quickly found one. In the indexes of some books on human sexuality we found the word "afterplay," and even a page or two about it.

Why only a few pages? Was this a highly technical concept that most people would not understand? Was it unimportant? We didn't think so, and private research among friends and colleagues confirmed what we suspected: that afterplay is neither technical nor trivial. "Afterplay" is a word that everyone can understand as describing a phenomenon that everyone who makes love experiences—and that nearly everyone realizes is important almost as soon as they hear the word. We knew that no one would say to us, "What, another book on afterplay?" But what helped keep us going was that no one said, "Who cares?"

Having realized that we were on to something, it was not until we ran a small preliminary study that we realized how significant the "something" was. This pilot investigation revealed not only that afterplay was important but that it might be the most important aspect of the sexual encounter. What we found in that study, and what we continued to find when we expanded the investigation to include hundreds of people, was that the success of a sexual relationship is more closely related to satisfaction with afterplay than with any other phase of the sexual encounter—foreplay, intercourse, even orgasm. (You'll find the statistical evidence in Chapter 7.)

And fewer people, we found, are satisfied with their afterplay than with any of the other phases. The reasons for this relative discontent became evident when we asked men and women what they did in the postintercourse period (Chapter 3) and compared the answers with what these same people said they liked (Chapter 5) and didn't like (Chapter 6).

We found out that, for the most part, men and women want the same things, and that what they want comes down to sensitivity and sharing. In a world populated with books like *Looking Out for Number One, How to Be Your Own Best Friend,* and *Pulling Your Own Strings,* most people told us that—at least after sex—they wanted their partners to look out for them, to be their best friends, to lie there with strings hopelessly entangled.

These desires are important ones. We found, when we asked people how they felt after sex, that many of us are unhappy, some miserable. But it is not true that depression must necessarily follow intercourse. In fact, some people experience a genuine "afterglow" (Chapter 4). Our own feeling about feelings is that they are not hard to change. And the main purpose of our book is to help you change yours. The changes in behavior that can enable anyone to experience the joys of afterplay will follow.

Afterplay is not a book for people interested in one-night stands or superficial relationships (although if you do the opposite of what we recommend, it might serve as a veritable handbook for such relationships). It is a book for men and women involved in a sexual relationship that is important to them or that seems to have the potential for importance. Nor is *Afterplay* a book for those who have major sexual problems. Today, more than ever before, extremely effective help is available to such people, and we recommend that you seek such help, if it's needed, before you read this book.

We are neither feminists nor "masculinists," but we did find that, until now, the significance of afterplay has been better understood by women than by men. One woman in her early thirties, when she heard of our results, put it very forcefully: "I think women have always known how important afterplay is. Many marriages have died because men don't." We found that women have experienced unpleasant—or nonexistent—afterplay more often than men, but there are many men who have had painful postcoital experiences. In any case, there are two of you in a relationship: What is bad for your partner is ultimately bad for you too.

If you are simply curious about afterplay, you will learn a lot from this book. Some stereotypes are supported, some are destroyed, and throughout the book you are bound to come across things you may never have thought about. If you think your relationship or your marriage could be better—or if you just *know* it could be—you will be satisfying more than curiosity when you read. You will be picking up valuable suggestions from the hundreds of Americans who contributed to this book.

One of these people is a woman whom we shall call Joanne S., a forty-one-year-old who appreciates things (and likes to express her appreciation), whether it be the countryside she sees from a car window, a piece of music, or another person. Relationships mean a great deal to her—not only with her husband, but with her family and close friends as well.

Four months ago Joanne was married for the second time, to a man who is thirteen years older and retired. They had been having a sexual relationship for nearly three years prior to their marriage. Joanne's only child, a son, no longer lives at home and thus she and her husband can have sex just about any time they choose. They make love frequently—most often at night or in the morning. The five to fifteen minutes they spend in foreplay are enough for Joanne, who has one or more orgasms most of the time. She appreciates her sexual experience—every part of it.

She is also very happy with her postintercourse experience. The moments after orgasm are as important to her as orgasm itself, and she believes that her husband feels the same way. She enjoys "snuggling" with him, and they "talk softly, kiss, hold each other, stroke and caress, joke, giggle." She feels "warm, female, loved, appreciated, relaxed, loving, fulfilled and in general very close to my man and really good about our life together." In describing their after-intercourse experience she says simply, "I love our closeness and lovingness."

On the rare occasions when one or both of them fails to reach orgasm, "we are no different than otherwise. We are together, and that's more important than an occasional misfire. We treat it with humor and love. There's always the next time." What she would not like after lovemaking—and does not get from her husband—is "to be criticized or chastised or left alone."

Joanne's final comment helps explain why this couple's sexual life is so satisfying to both of them: "A good sense of humor is vital to a good relationship. If kids could be taught to be less grim about sex, they would be less hung up throughout their lives. Loving and laughing go together."

Does it matter what you do after sex? The authors of today's books and articles don't seem to think so. They slowly and titillatingly guide us through the growing excitement of foreplay. Next, they graphically describe (and, often, colorfully illustrate) the many positions of love. Finally, they attempt to describe the indescribable, the human orgasm. And there they leave us.

But life goes on after orgasm. For many of us, in fact, it does not so much go on as flood in. All of the experts, all our experience, all our books never quite prepare us for that inevitable moment: the end of the orgasm. If we allow ourselves to be jarred out of sex just as we allow the alarm to jar us from sleep—or if, exhausted, we immediately go to sleep—we are missing the benefits and pleasures of afterplay.

You probably have your own idea of what the word "afterplay" means. (We're assuming that no one believes this to be a book about posttheater etiquette.) Since the latest edition of *Webster's Unabridged* does not even include the word, we offer this definition: *Afterplay is whatever you do and whatever happens to you after sex.* Contained in the word itself is the idea that afterplay is an inevitable sequel to play. Unlike some inevitable sequels, afterplay is not only not fearsome, it is naturally enjoyable.

Orgasm, Sleep, and Consciousness

Next to sleep, intercourse and orgasm are the most profound changes in consciousness most human beings ever experience. Like sleep, intercourse has a beginning and end. Or, put a little differently, it has an entrance and an exit. We know a lot about these entrances: how to fall asleep, how to initiate lovemaking. But we are primitive in our knowledge of the exits. We don't know the best ways to awaken and are perhaps even more ignorant in our knowledge of how to emerge from orgasm and intercourse.

But there is a very good chance that how we make our exits is as important as how we make our entrances. In fact we acknowledge, at least superstitiously, that the way we exit from sleep may have important implications for the whole day. ("I woke up on the wrong side of the bed today!") As for our exits from orgasm and intercourse, we haven't acknowledged anything.

How people wake up probably does affect their daytime moods and actions, but we will leave that topic to others. We have concentrated on exits from lovemaking. Although few psychologists have had much, if anything, to say about the postintercourse period, few would deny that orgasm *and* its aftermath are genuine altered states. As such, they are equally worthy of study.

What About the Sex Researchers?

Back in 1953, Alfred Kinsey, the Indiana biologist who dragged American sexual activity out of the bedroom (along with the many other locations he discovered people were using for sex), had this to say about the postorgasmic period: "For most persons who have experienced orgasm there is . . . a quiescence, a calm, a peace, a satisfaction with the world which, in the minds of many persons, is the most notable aspect of sexual activity."[1] No one in the field of human sexuality seems to have taken much interest in Kinsey's provocative comment. This is understandable in light of the fascination surrounding everything that comes before orgasm. And yet, given Kinsey's preeminence, it is a little shocking to see what incredibly short shrift afterplay has received in recent sexual literature: about six pages in Masters and Johnson's *Human Sexual Response* and less than three pages in *Human Sexual Inadequacy*; four pages in *The Hite Report* and in *The Sensuous Man*; two pages in *Becoming Orgasmic*; one page in *The Sensuous Woman*; and, finally, a grand total of zero pages in *Everything You Always Wanted to Know* and *The Joy of Sex*, two of the most popular books in the history of manandwomankind.

Why Has Afterplay Been Ignored?

None of the researchers on sex have actually said that afterplay is unimportant. They have simply ignored it. We can only speculate as to why:

• Perhaps the postcoital period is simply not a special or unique time. There is, according to this perspective, no way to discriminate between postintercourse time and any other kind of time in people's lives. And even if postintercourse behavior and experience are somewhat different from the usual, they are not sufficiently different to deserve special attention.

• Considering the tremendous excitement and activity surrounding foreplay, intercourse, and orgasm, afterplay simply pales by comparison. It is not interesting. Why bother with it?

• Orgasm can best be understood as a release of psychological and physiological tension. Once tension is released, the sexual partners are in a state of rest and relaxation. There is nothing important about a state of equilibrium.

• From a biological point of view, the species-preserving function is accomplished with the male orgasm. Sexual behavior should therefore be studied beginning with foreplay and concluding with the ejaculation of sperm into the vagina.

• Why study what happens after sex? We all know what happens. People all do the same thing. It is late, we are drowsy, we go to sleep.

We suggest that you reserve judgment on the nature, importance, and function of afterplay. For in reading this book you may discover—as did we—that afterplay can be easily discriminated from any other period in human experience; that the activities surrounding afterplay may equal or surpass the satisfactions of foreplay, intercourse, and orgasm; that there may be a special significance in the state of consciousness that characterizes afterplay; that from a biological point of view, the species-preserving function of bonding and sharing may be at its peak in the moments following intercourse; that people do not all do the same things after sex, and they do not all fall asleep.

In our view, afterplay has been disregarded *because of its special and important qualities*. It is a time of heightened vulnerability and openness. Many people fear communication and sharing; they are afraid of closeness and intimacy. They would prefer to close their eyes to afterplay.

Afterplay: The Last Frontier?

The door that Kinsey and his coauthors opened a crack in the late 1940s has since swung open wide. Beginning with the famous Kinsey Reports of 1948 and 1953 (the actual titles were *Sexual Behavior in the Human Male* and *Human Female*, respectively), we have seen an inundation of information on what Americans do, or say they do, in their bedrooms. *The Hite Report* of 1976 is the logical sequel to Kinsey. The descriptive language has changed,[*] but we are still being told what everyone else is doing sexually. And still we are fascinated.

And yet something has been missing—namely, information on what people do *after* intercourse. There are jokes about rolling over and going to sleep, but how many people actually do it? What proportion of people enjoy staying in physical contact after sex? And how many actually avoid such contact? Is conversation, sharing, and intimacy the norm or do more people prefer to smoke a cigarette or watch television? And, finally, what are some of the less usual things that people do in that state Robert Penn Warren has called the "strangely therapeutic post-coital languor"?[2]

---

[*] For example, compare Kinsey's description of clitoral masturbation with that of the Hite Report.(The excerpt from Hite is actually a quote from an anonymous respondent). Kinsey (1953): "In masturbation, the female usually moves a finger gently or rhythmically over the sensitive areas, or applies a rhythmic pressure with her whole hand. Frequently a single finger or two may be slowly or more rapidly moved forward between the labia in a manner which brings each stroke against the clitoris" (p. 159). Hite Report (1976): "I masturbate in bed with the door shut (four roommates). First, I lean a pillow against my bed and sit in a reading position. I put a dab of vaseline on my clitoris, and get some pornographic literature (maybe a questionnaire!) and then I spread my legs a little and begin to gently rub back and forth on my clitoris with my index finger. I become excited, stop reading and turn out the light, take off my glasses. Then I return to more rapid back and forth rubbing on my clitoris and fantasize, then I orgasm. I continue to rub my clitoris until it is over. Usually my knees are bent up with my left hand gripping the edge of the mattress as pelvic thrusts increase in intensity, sometimes closing my legs on my hand and rolling onto my side and rubbing my clitoris" (p. 23).

The Importance of Afterplay

Our research into American afterplay has produced many fascinating personal accounts of what people do after sex. But the most significant finding concerns the importance of afterplay in a couple's sexual relationship as a whole.

With all the foreplay "techniques" so amply described, the positions during intercourse diagrammed and discussed and illustrated in such detail, it is not clear that there has been a corresponding increase in satisfaction with sexual relationships. In fact, it would seem that the more we learn of sexual techniques the worse off are our relationships. In 1975, more than one million couples were divorced, twice as many as in 1960 and three times as many as in 1950. Between 1970 and 1975, the number of people under 35 maintaining a household alone *doubled* from 1.5 to three million.[3]

Perhaps the emphasis on sexual techniques has been at the expense of emphasis on the more human aspects of sex, aspects which are never nearer the surface than in the postintercourse period.

Improving Yourself and Your Relationship

Human beings are uniquely capable of helping themselves and each other to grow. Through greater self-awareness, knowledge, and the willingness to change, we can dramatically improve our relationships. The improvement is not likely to be brought about by making love on the kitchen floor, or by performing gymnastic feats. Assuming the pretzel position may be good for the spine, but it is no replacement for sharing and communication in the development of a relationship.

The period following lovemaking is a time of relaxed awareness and heightened sensitivity, a time centered in the present. As such, it plays a significant part in determining how often we have sex and how happy we are with our sexual relationship. It is a special time which, if not ignored, can be used to improve a relationship overall and make us more whole.

Your problems today could be due less to which side of the bed you woke up on this morning than to which side you fell onto last night. We are interested in the aspect of sexual activity that occurs in every sexual encounter and is critical in determining sexual and total satisfaction—the ending, which for us is the beginning.

CHAPTER 2

Finding Out

Most of us are interested in what goes through the minds of other people, and in what they are doing. Psychologists are different only in that they are perhaps a bit more curious and are interested in understanding the connections among the different aspects of a person. If psychologists do know any more than anyone else about why we are the way we are, it is only to the extent that they have satisfied some of this curiosity. They have done so not only through reading, research, and clinical practice, but by observing and questioning friends, relatives, acquaintances, and, of course, themselves.

We have used all of the above in our study of American afterplay. But our reliance on information gained from clinical practice was minimal. We were primarily interested in the afterplay experience of basically healthy people. Our book therefore speaks for, and to, such people—who, after all, make up the vast majority of human beings.

The Questionnaire

The major source of our data was a questionnaire, which we hope you will fill out, either mentally or on a sheet of paper, before reading the rest of this book. Not only will this enable you to empathize with the nearly two hundred fifty people in our sample, but it will, when you see their responses in the chapters ahead, permit you to compare your own answers to theirs.

If you simply skim the questionnaire, *please* stop to read questions 40 through 45—carefully. Responses to these questions are the basis for most of our conclusions about afterplay.

RESEARCH QUESTIONNAIRE ON HUMAN SEXUALITY

The purpose of this research is to obtain information about the sexual behaviors and experiences of adult males and females. Beginning with the work of Kinsey, there have been a number of systematic investigations of human sexuality. The primary purpose of the present project is to explore the relationships between behavior and experience before, during, and after sexual intercourse.

Your participation in this research is, of course, voluntary. We do request that if you choose to take part in this scientific investigation, you be *complete, thorough,* and *honest.* YOUR RESPONSES WILL REMAIN COMPLETELY ANONYMOUS. IN FACT, WE MUST INSIST THAT YOU OMIT THE MENTION OF ANY NAMES, PLACES OR DATES IN YOUR RESPONSES TO THESE OFTEN HIGHLY PERSONAL QUESTIONS.

Please return the completed questionnaire in the stamped and addressed envelope that has been provided (do not put your return address on this envelope). We would very much appreciate receiving the questionnaire as soon as possible (at least within two weeks).

Thank you very much for your cooperation.

Unless specific information is requested, please place an "X" or check mark in the appropriate space. Feel free to qualify any of your answers in the available space.

1. Your sex: Male _____   Female _X_____

2. Your age: _____

3. How many children do you have living with you? __O___

4. Your principal occupation: _____

5. Are you presently having sexual relations with one or more persons (involving having sex at least once a month)?

$$Yes \underline{\quad X \quad} \qquad No \underline{\qquad}$$

If your answer to Question 5 is *Yes*, please provide the characteristics of your principal partner in Questions 6–8 below. If you have no principal partner or your answer is *No*, describe your most recent partner in Questions 6–8 below. Please refer to the person described below when answering other questions in this questionnaire.

6. Sex of your partner: Male _X_____   Female _____

7. Partner's age: _____

8. Partner's principal occupation: _____

9. Are you and your partner: Married ___Not living together ___
   Living together (but not married) _____
   Other (please specify) _____

10. How long have you had (or did you have) a sexual relationship with this partner? (Use days, weeks, months, or years—whichever is most appropriate): _____

11. Are you currently involved in sexual relations with more than one person?

Yes _____   No __X____

12. At what time of day do you engage in sex? Please indicate the most typical time of day by marking a "1," the next most typical by marking a "2," the next a "3," and the least typical by a "4."

Morning __/__   Afternoon __3__
Evening __2__   Night __/__

13. What method or methods of contraception do you and your partner typically use? _____

14. How much time do you and your partner typically spend in foreplay behavior?

Less than 5 min. ____   5–15 min. ____
15–30 min. __X__   30 min. or more ____

15. How much time would you *like* to devote to foreplay, relative to the amount of time you actually do spend?
Much more ____ Somewhat more ____ The same __X__
Somewhat less ____ Much less ____

16. To what extent are you satisfied with your typical foreplay experience?
Very satisfied __X__ Satisfied ____ Somewhat satisfied ____
Somewhat dissatisfied ____Dissatisfied ____Very dissatisfied ____

17. Approximately how many times per week do you and your partner engage in sex?
Less than once a week __Once a week __2–3 times a week_X_
4–6 times per week ____ More than 6 times per week ____

18. How often would you *like* to have sex, relative to how often you actually do?
Much more often ___ Somewhat more often ___ The same _X_
Somewhat less often ___ Much less often ___

19. Approximately what percentage of the times you have sex do you reach orgasm?
(Please indicate a percentage between 0 and 100): _100_ %

20. How many orgasms do you have during a typical lovemaking session? _3_

21. How satisfied are you with your experience during actual intercourse?
Very satisfied _X_ Satisfied ___ Somewhat satisfied ___
Somewhat dissatisfied ___ Dissatisfied ___ Very dissatisfied ___

22. How satisfied do you think your partner is with his/her experience during actual intercourse?
Very satisfied _X_ Satisfied ___ Somewhat satisfied ___
Somewhat dissatisfied ___ Dissatisfied ___ Very dissatisfied ___

23. Do you fall asleep directly after intercourse?
Never or almost never ___ Sometimes ___ About half the time _X_
Usually ___ Almost always or always ___

24. Does your partner fall asleep directly after intercourse?
Never or almost never ___ Sometimes ___ About half the time ___
Usually _X_ Almost always or always ___

25. Immediately after intercourse, do you prefer to be physically separated from (i.e., not touching) your partner?
Never or almost never _X_ Sometimes ___ About half the time ___
Usually ___ Almost always or always ___

26. Immediately after intercourse, does your partner prefer to be physically separated from (i.e., not touching) you?

Never or almost never __X__Sometimes __About half the time __
Usually ___Almost always or always ___

27. For how long a time do you and your partner typically remain in physical contact after intercourse (e.g., hugging, caressing): (Indicate approximate number of minutes—do not include contact while sleeping): __1/2 hr_____

28. How often do you praise your partner after intercourse?
Never or almost never __X__Sometimes __About half the time __
Usually __ Almost always or always __

29. How often does your partner praise you after intercourse?
Never or almost never __X__Sometimes __About half the time __
Usually __ Almost always or always __

30. How often do you speak romantically to your partner after intercourse?
Never or almost never __Sometimes __X__About half the time __
Usually __ Almost always or always __

31. How often does your partner speak romantically to you after intercourse?
Never or almost never __Sometimes __X__About half the time __
Usually ___ Almost always or always ___

32. How satisfied are you with your typical *post*-intercourse experience?
Very satisfied ___ Satisfied __X__ Somewhat satisfied ___
Somewhat dissatisfied ___Dissatisfied ___Very dissatisfied ___

33. How satisfied do you think your partner is with his/her typical post-intercourse experience?
Very satisfied ___ Satisfied __X__ Somewhat satisfied ___
Somewhat dissatisfied ___Dissatisfied ___Very dissatisfied ___

34. Using the scale below, indicate the level of importance you

place on each of the following periods of sexual experience by marking a number in each blank (each number may be used more than once).

1	2	3	4	5
Totally Unimportant				Very Important

Foreplay ___ Intercourse ___ Orgasm ___
The 5 minutes after orgasm ___ The next hour ___

35. Using the scale above, indicate the level of importance you think your partner would place on each of the following periods of sexual experience by marking a number in each blank (as before, each number may be used more than once).

Foreplay ___ Intercourse ___ Orgasm ___
The 5 minutes after orgasm ___ The next hour ___

36. In general, how satisfied are you with your sexual relationship with your partner?
Very satisfied ___ Satisfied ___ Somewhat satisfied ___
Somewhat dissatisfied ___ Dissatisfied ___ Very dissatisfied ___

37. In general, how satisfied do you think your partner is with his/her sexual relationship with you?
Very satisfied ___ Satisfied ___ Somewhat satisfied ___
Somewhat dissatisfied ___ Dissatisfied ___ Very dissatisfied ___

38. How satisfied are you with your *overall* relationship with your partner?
Very satisfied ___ Satisfied ___ Somewhat satisfied _X_
Somewhat dissatisfied ___ Dissatisfied ___ Very dissatisfied ___

39. How satisfied do you think your partner is with his/her *overall* relationship with you?
Very satisfied _X_ Satisfied ___ Somewhat satisfied _X_
Somewhat dissatisfied ___ Dissatisfied ___ Very dissatisfied ___

40. Describe *what you do and how you feel* directly after intercourse and for the next half hour or so.

41. Describe what you would consider the ideal after-intercourse experience. Include: the kind of atmosphere and activities you like; and the kinds of things you like or would like your partner to say and do right after you have had sex.

42. Describe what you would consider a negative after-intercourse experience. Include: the kinds of things you do not like or would not like your partner to say and do after you have had sex.

43. Practically everyone has at least occasional difficulties in sex (premature ejaculation, failure to reach orgasm, etc.). What do you say or do just after your partner has had such difficulties?

44. Below are listed some activities in which people might engage in the hour following intercourse. Please indicate the fre-

quency with which you typically engage in each of these activities. Feel free to add any additional activities to the list. Use the following scale to indicate frequency:

0 – Never   3 – About half of the time
1 – Infrequently   4 – Often
2 – Sometimes   5 – Always

___ Sleep
___ Converse with partner
___ Get something to eat at home
___ Go out to eat
___ Watch TV
___ Read
___ Wash up
___ Go to work
___ Give massage

___ Receive massage
___ Socialize with others
___ Drink an alcoholic beverage
___ Smoke a cigarette
___ Have more sex
___ Listen to music
___ Run an errand
___ Go to the bathroom
___ Other (please specify)

45. If you have comments about this questionnaire or about any aspects of your sexual experience which you feel are important, feel free to write these comments in the space provided below. We are especially interested in any unusual postintercourse experience, positive or negative.

You may have wondered why there were questions about other parts of the sexual encounter—foreplay, intercourse, orgasm. They were included because we wanted to find out how afterplay fits into the whole sexual experience. For example, we wanted to know how important it is when compared to orgasm. (See Chapter 7 for the answer to this and other similar questions.)

And you may have noticed that we frequently used the word

"satisfied" ("How satisfied are you with . . . ?"). Some recent questionnaires, distributed nationally, have not used the word at all. Why not? We suspect that the reason is an implicit assumption that satisfaction equals orgasm. We made no such assumption and, in fact, our data indicate that although orgasms are certainly involved in satisfaction, one does not equal the other.

The Sample

Most of what we learned about American afterplay came from the 234 questionnaires filled out and sent back to us anonymously. Since we distributed approximately 850, the return rate was a little over 25 percent. Compared to other recent studies of human sexuality this rate is quite high. A sample of this size is considerably larger than the sample sizes of most psychological studies. However, the representativeness of the sample is much more important than the numbers. A sample of one million participants selected because they are members of singles clubs, or any other clubs, would not give us as accurate a picture of American afterplay as a few hundred people of different ages and occupations selected from various parts of the country.

Our sample was highly varied. Men and women of various ages and occupations, living in different parts of the country, were carefully selected to distribute the questionnaire to people in their social and occupational milieu. One hundred forty-one women and ninety-three men sent them back; thus women represented 60 percent of the sample. Only one respondent in nine was living with, but not married to, his or her partner. The others were evenly divided between married and single. Ages ranged from 17 to 63, with an average age of 30 (28 for women; 32 for men).

The respondents were from all over the United States, although a majority came from the east and west coasts. Postmarks showed that questionnaires were sent back from the following states: California, Colorado, Connecticut, Indiana,

Maine, Massachusetts, New Hampshire, New Jersey, New York, Ohio, Pennsylvania, Rhode Island, Tennessee, Texas, and Washington. The most (67) came from the state of New York, and next was California (50).

Our sample was most diverse with respect to occupations or areas of employment. Respondents listed a total of 83, namely:

Accountant
Actor
Actress
Administrator
Advertising
Assistant Professor
Associate Professor
Audio-Visual Technician
Banker
Book Publisher
Bookkeeper
Business
Business Analyst
Business Executive
Carpenter
Child Care Worker
Cinematographer
Clerk/Typist
Clinician
Collections
Composer
Computer Analyst
Computer Professional
Consultant
Controller
Corporation President
Counselor
Dancer
Editor
Educational Administration

Electrician
Engineer
Entertainer
File Clerk
Film Editor
Free Lance Researcher
Free Lance Writer
Hospital Technician
Housewife/Homemaker
Human Services Worker
Instructor
Journalist
Lawyer
Legal Secretary
Librarian
Library Clerk
Medical Researcher
Mental Health Worker
Merchandising
Mother
Municipal Clerk
Musician
Office Manager
Office Worker
Pharmacist
Photographer
Physical Therapist
Physician
Podiatrist
Psychologist

Psychologist Intern
Quality Control Supervisor
Receptionist
Registered Nurse
Reporter
Retailer
Retired
Salesman
Secretary
Secretary/Bookkeeper
Social Worker
Sociologist

Special Education Teacher
Stewardess
Stock Market
Student
Systems Management
Teacher
Theater
Technical Illustrator
Travel Agent
TV Producer
Writer

The occupations (professional, student, etc.) were roughly the same for both sexes, and in general the men and women came from the same geographic areas and the same socioeconomic milieu.

We found a number of people whose stories show a wide range of postintercourse experiences and types of relationships. The story of one of these, Joanne S., has already been presented. The others will be found throughout the book. With the exception of a few details changed to prevent identification and the adding of fictitious names, these "case studies" are based entirely on responses to the questionnaire. In fact, for each person's story, the title we chose was a quote from his or her responses.

CHAPTER 3

What People Do

When we began work on this project, several friends and colleagues with whom we discussed it seemed to feel that there was nothing to study. More than once our mention of the postintercourse period was met with a nervous laugh and a comment like this one from a woman in her late thirties: "What is there to study? Doesn't everybody just sleep?"

Some authors of recent books on human sexuality appear to share this view, which could explain why these texts contain little if any information about afterplay. Also, like many laypersons, these authors have assumed that in the male in particular there is a strong tendency to sleep after sex. Eric T. Pengelley in *Sex and Human Life*, a college textbook published in 1974, refers to the "male's natural desire to relax and sleep" after his orgasm; he goes on to say that, in both sexes, following orgasm "there is an almost universal urge to sleep."[1] In her highly respected work *The New Sex Therapy*, also published in

1974, Dr. Helen Singer Kaplan writes that the male "often feels placid and sleepy after intercourse."[2]

Does nearly everybody—or at least everybody male—just "roll over and go to sleep" after sex? Our research yielded a clear reply: Many men and women do not go right to sleep after sex; in fact, some people feel energized rather than enervated. Among them is a 37-year-old college professor who said he often felt exhilarated and after a short rest was sometimes able to "grade four hours of research papers in 45 minutes," to which he added, "Wow!"

When people do not go to sleep directly after intercourse, what *do* they do? It turns out that there is at least as much variety possible in afterplay as there is in foreplay and intercourse.

For instance, perhaps you like to read after sex. More than half the people we surveyed said they do, at least occasionally, and for some reading was a standard part of their afterplay. Are you by any chance in the postintercourse period right now? If so, that is all right as long as you and your partner are happy. But if you have just had sex and are reading as a second choice because your partner is alseep, you might at some point show him—it *is* more likely to be a "him"—the pages that follow, if not the whole book.

In those pages you'll find a survey of what Americans do after they have sex. The first three sections cover the most common behavior among the people in our sample; the ones that follow are in approximate order of frequency.

Sleep

> —the innocent sleep,
> Sleep that knits up the ravel'd sleave of care,
> The death of each day's life, sore labour's bath,
> Balm of hurt minds, great nature's second course,
> Chief nourisher in life's feast.
> —William Shakespeare (1564–1616)
> *Macbeth*, Act II, Scene 2

Our research turned up no natural connection between sex and sleep in either males or females—which leads us to wonder whether sleep after sex doesn't indicate that the lovemaking itself may be a "sore labor" or have left one or both partners with a "hurt mind." Certainly going to sleep right after sex may be a result of the late hour at which many people begin lovemaking. Many of us give lovemaking a very low priority in our lives and do not get to it until late at night, if we get to it at all.

There is a common misconception that sleep is a physiological necessity, the all but inevitable conclusion to sex. Yet if sleep "had" to follow intercourse, we would expect to find that everyone, or practically everyone slept after sex. The first thing we learned from our questions on sleeping was that this is simply not so. Sleep, though certainly a common experience during the postcoital period, is anything but the universal afterplay many of us suppose it to be.

Let's see how common it actually is. To begin with, just how frequently do people "roll over and go to sleep" in the moments immediately following lovemaking? Consider the responses to Question 23.

DO YOU FALL ASLEEP DIRECTLY AFTER INTERCOURSE?

	Percentages	
Response	Men	*Women*
Never or almost never	30.1	34.5
Sometimes	34.4	39.6
About half the time	17.2	8.6
Usually	16.1	11.5
Always or almost always	2.2	5.8

Looking at the first two lines of numbers—which give the percentage of our respondents for whom immediate sleep is infrequent—you can see that sleep is not inextricably bound up with sex. The last three lines, on the other hand, make it clear that significant percentages of men (36 percent) and women (26 percent) do go to sleep immediately after intercourse at least half the time. For these people, sleep is their most typical afterplay experience. In addition, males are more likely to fall asleep than females—here our data support the sexual stereotype.

If you think about it, you will realize that sleep is a strange behavior. One of the strangest things about it is that you are usually not aware of the moment when it begins. It is almost impossible to remember exactly when you fell asleep; you may think you were awake at a given moment when it was clear to an observer that you were sleeping. For this reason we considered the responses to Question 24 to be particularly important.

DOES YOUR PARTNER FALL ASLEEP DIRECTLY AFTER INTERCOURSE?

	Percentages	
Response	Men	Women
Never or almost never	29.0	23.2
Sometimes	37.6	37.7
About half the time	19.4	7.2
Usually	9.7	23.2
Always or almost always	4.3	8.7

Reports by partners put the percentages of people who, at least half the time, simply "roll over" after sex at even higher levels (33 percent for women, 39 percent for men). We are not, it seems, always aware of the fact when our immediate response to the end of intercourse is sleep.

Perhaps your response to these findings is simply to shrug your shoulders or doze off. But let's stop for a minute to consider the significance of this behavior. Roughly averaging the responses to Questions 23 and 24, we can see that approximately one third of the questionnaire's respondents are immediately and abruptly isolated from their partners following sex. Sleep is the most separate and isolating form of consciousness we commonly enter. Freud called it "a condition in which I refuse to have anything to do with the outer world and have withdrawn interest from it."[3] Certainly the afterplay (if it can even be called that) of those of us who do go to sleep immediately, is unconscious—we share nothing with our partners except perhaps an occasional snore. We have entered a world completely separate from our lovers, a world in which we exist incommunicado.

The following case shows how far removed sharing and intimacy can be from "good" sex. Even Mr. T's waking fantasy is an activity which in no way involves his partner.

I go to sleep

George T., an attorney, is 36 years old and has been married to a writer for 12 years. They have five children. Mr. T. says he is satisfied with his marital and sexual relationship. He and his wife have sex about once a week. Although he believes the time following sex to be important for his wife, it is not important for him, and he prefers to be physically separated from his wife right after intercourse. He and his wife never express affection or compliment each other after sex. In fact, any kind of talk is unlikely since they both always go to sleep directly after intercourse.

Mr. T.'s fantasy of the ideal postintercourse experience would be to have "five 18-year-old women come in and lick me clean." What he would like least would be to have his partner laugh at him. He reports that his actual postintercourse behavior is unvarying, whether he is with his wife or another sexual partner (he has had a number of affairs), "I go to sleep," he says, "regardless of the time of day."

If Mr. T.'s attitude sounds anything like your partner's, and you do not find it appealing, you are not alone. As we will see in later chapters, many people feel that having a partner fall asleep immediately following sex is unsatisfactory at the very least.

Falling asleep immediately limits afterplay to this single activity. But how many of us fall asleep some time later after we have made love? We asked Question 44 to find out.

HOW OFTEN DO YOU SLEEP IN THE HOUR FOLLOWING
INTERCOURSE?

Response	Percentages* Men	Women
Never	5.6	2.9
Infrequently	7.9	12.2
Sometimes	24.7	28.1
About half the time	23.6	18.7
Often	33.7	32.4
Always	4.5	5.8

The results suggest a number of things, some more clearly than others. First of all, it becomes apparent once again that sleep, even an hour after intercourse, is not the universal result of sex. However, a majority of us do fall asleep sometime within the hour. Obviously there is no single explanation for this behavior. Sexual activity is often strenuous—for many of us it is the only exercise we get—and orgasm in particular makes great demands on the physiological resources of the body. These demands, and the late hour at which many of us engage in sex, can serve to bring on sleep. But in addition to these physical explanations, there may be other reasons for sleep after sex. It may be a retreat from emotion and intimacy—a psychological as well as a physical refuge. We will explore the implications of this reaction to sex in the next chapter.

*Due to rounding off, percentages may not add up to exactly 100.0.

The results for this question are somewhat ambiguous for the simple reason that there is a span of time involved. We do not know how many people fall asleep after a few minutes, how many after a full hour. Obviously this quantitative difference has qualitative implications. The more time there is between sleep and sex, the more possibilities there are for afterplay. If you always fall asleep immediately, you have obviously chosen to severely limit the kind of contact and communication you can have with your partner. The more time you choose to give yourself, the more possibilities you open up. Of course it is *how* you choose to fill your time together that is of the greatest importance. Going to sleep immediately is surely preferable to spending an hour in argument.

But sleep in and of itself, like most human behaviors, cannot be evaluated as good or bad in absolute terms. For some of us sleep can be a pleasant postcoital activity.

I get as close to my husband as possible. I just relax and lie in his arms. I feel warm and contented. I fall asleep in his arms. (woman, 47)

However, for others, sleep reflects discontent and even hostility.

What I did was to move over to my side of the bed because he always went right to sleep and didn't like being touched except in direct connection to the sex act. (woman, 26)

I usually wish it could have been better but realize it could have been worse. I usually fall asleep directly after. (woman, 31)

In either case, if our afterplay is always limited to sleep, no matter how pleasant, we are definitely missing something. Perhaps we opt for sleep only because we haven't given much thought to the alternatives. If you are one of those people who just "roll over" after sex, read on and find out what some of us are doing while you're sleeping.

Maintain Physical Contact

I want to be touched . . . I want to touch and gently kiss him, never being physically separated from him. (woman, 23)

One of the most famous studies in psychology involves infant rhesus monkeys. In the 1950s Harry Harlow, at the University of Wisconsin, tested the theory that the attachment between mother and child comes from the feeding situation—that the mother, as the source of nourishment, becomes an object of love. Of course, feeding is inextricably bound up with touching and holding, and in the human situation one cannot experiment with this. Harlow reared infant monkeys in cages with two types of "surrogate mothers"—one was a vaguely monkey-looking wire mesh set-up with a bottle inside it and a nipple sticking out from its "chest." The infant could only feed from this "mother." Next to the wire mother was a similar contraption covered with soft terry cloth; "she" had neither bottle nor nipple. Harlow found that the infant monkey spent far more time holding the cloth mother—and ran to it, not to the feeding wire mother, when frightened. His conclusion, which was supported by further research, was that the critical variable in the development of parent-child affection is not the supplying of nourishment but is what he called "contact comfort."

Many people understandably question the ethics of treating monkeys or any other animals this way, and we sincerely hope no one would ever carry out this kind of experiment with humans. But nature, unfortunately, has done some experiments on her own. Until relatively recently, orphaned babies were reared in rather sterile environments with little human attention and contact. Many of these babies developed what has been called "institutional retardation." Other research has indicated that babies and children who are not touched by parents at home are likely to develop serious psychological problems.

The case from this empirical evidence is strong—human

beings, like other animals, require physical contact to develop into healthy and whole adults.

Sex cannot help but bring people physically together. While it is generally not enough in itself to keep people together, it should naturally reinforce any potentially good relationship. People's bodies feel good to us and feel better to the extent that we care for them: It *is* worth taking the advice of bumper stickers and TV commercials that suggest you hug your child—not only is it good for your child, but it feels good too. The embrace of a close friend is also pleasurable in a special way. Even a handshake may be a significant event—its significance becomes obvious when an expected hand is not proffered.

But intercourse is in a class by itself. Not only is there the most intimate of contact, but there is more of it than in any other human interaction. It is not merely our hands that touch, nor even just the genitals. There is prolonged full body contact, which for many people is one of the most pleasurable aspects of intercourse. Our question was, does this contact continue to feel good after one or both partners has had an orgasm, or does it become aversive?

We phrased Question 25 in an extreme form. We wanted to know if anyone preferred *immediate* separation.

IMMEDIATELY AFTER INTERCOURSE
DO YOU PREFER TO BE PHYSICALLY
SEPARATED FROM (I.E., NOT TOUCHING)
YOUR PARTNER?

	Percentages	
Response	*Men*	*Women*
Never or almost never	58.1	75.9
Sometimes	31.2	19.9
About half the time	5.4	0.7
Usually	5.4	2.1
Almost always or always	0	1.4

Although a majority of both sexes do prefer continued physical closeness after intercourse, the preference is stronger in women. More than 75 percent of women never want immediate physical separation, as opposed to less than 60 percent of the men. Incidentally, the woman's preference to remain in contact with her partner had nothing to do with her orgasmic experience. That is, there was no relationship whatsoever between the percentage of time orgasm was reached, or number of orgasms typically achieved, and the woman's desire for continued closeness.

We also asked respondents to tell us how they thought their partners felt about separating directly after sex.

IMMEDIATELY AFTER INTERCOURSE
DOES YOUR PARTNER PREFER TO BE
PHYSICALLY SEPARATED FROM (I.E., NOT TOUCHING) YOU?

	Percentages	
Response	Men	Women
Never or almost never	64.5	60.0
Sometimes	31.2	27.0
About half the time	1.1	4.3
Usually	2.2	6.4
Always or almost always	1.1	2.1

The women in our sample were remarkably accurate in their perceptions of their partner's preference for physical separation. The men, on the other hand, slightly underestimated women's needs for continued contact.

Although some people reported that direct genital stimulation following orgasm can be a bit painful, the vast majority do not prefer immediate and total physical separation. But let's look into this aspect of afterplay a little more closely: Does the desire not to separate grow out of a desire for physical contact and warmth, or more out of an inability to move apart? We were somewhat optimistic about the state of American afterplay when we learned that most people disliked immediate separation. Our optimism soured somewhat when we saw for how long the physical contact was maintained. Perhaps the preference for continued contact came not from a need for maintaining intimacy but rather from a need to recoup energies momentarily lost in the exertions of sex. Certainly the answers we got to Question 27 would suggest so.

FOR HOW LONG A TIME DO YOU AND YOUR PARTNER TYPICALLY REMAIN IN PHYSICAL CONTACT AFTER INTERCOURSE (HUGGING, CARESSING)? (INDICATE APPROXIMATE NUMBER OF MINUTES—DO NOT INCLUDE CONTACT WHILE SLEEPING)

	Percentages	
Response	Men	Women
0–5 minutes	23.9	25.7
6–10 minutes	21.7	25.0
11–15 minutes	12.0	18.6
16–20 minutes	17.4	7.1
21–25 minutes	2.2	2.1
26–30 minutes	16.3	12.1
31–35 minutes	0	0.7
36–40 minutes	2.2	2.9
over 40 minutes	4.3	5.7

Almost half our respondents spend ten minutes or less in physical contact, and nearly one person in four spends five minutes or less. Five minutes or less! We realize that it is possible that love and warmth can be communicated in five minutes, but it seems likely that most people who spend this minimal amount of time on contact are probably "coming down" from the exertion of intercourse. Five minutes of contact is likely to mean getting the energy to move away.

Physical contact is certainly preferable to separation. But as we shall see, people who do spend time in physical contact are not necessarily involved actively and intimately. Clearly the quality of the contact is as or more important than the quantity. For some, unfortunately, long periods of postcoital physical contact means lying on top of one another while their minds drift elsewhere.

In Question 44 we did not ask about physical contact in general, but about a particular kind of contact: massage. Massage is a special kind of touching, which may involve the rubbing or kneading of another person's body. By asking how many people give or receive massage in the postintercourse period, we were trying to get some measure of the quality of contact. Are people in contact after sex likely to be actively touching and caressing each other or is their contact completely passive? Consider the responses to our question on the frequency of massage.

	Percentages	
Response	Men	Women
Never	35.2	36.2
Infrequently	19.3	25.4
Sometimes	30.7	28.3
About half the time	11.4	5.8
Often	2.3	4.3
Always	1.1	0

Massage is a very frequent part of afterplay for less than five percent of our sample; for more than a third it is *never* a part of it. But as you will see, massage was mentioned by a sizeable number of people as an element in ideal afterplay, and it was never mentioned by anyone as an unpleasant postintercourse element. So if you feel that you would like more active, more extended, touching after sex, you are not alone.

In their responses to Question 40, where people were asked to describe their activities, more people mentioned some kind of physical contact than anything else. But the kind of touching and the way it was described differed considerably depending on whether or not the person was satisfied with his or her relationship.

The following responses were given by very satisfied people:

Very tender toward mate. Very desirous of kissing and touching her neck, face, breasts. (man, 49)

I remain on top of or beside or next to him. I usually kiss, hug and tell him how good it was. (woman, 28)

I cuddle and am very affectionate and like to be petted and held close. (woman, 24)

I like to lay still and squeeze him in my arms, touch him and feel his penis in my vagina as I flex my vaginal muscles. (woman, 33)

After sex we hug each other and kiss and tell each other how good it felt and how much we love each other. (man, 23)

I feel like being close together is so special, I usually give him hugs and kisses, and sometimes just squeeze him. Then we lie together— sometimes face to face with our bodies very close, sometimes on our backs touching at different parts of the body, sometimes on our sides with either my arm around his waist or his around mine, and sometimes I lie on top of him. (woman, 18)

I feel relaxed and lazy and full. My partner usually stays inside me for a while and we caress each other quietly. As we start getting more energy, we "play" more as our caresses turn to tickles. We roll around the bed (and sometimes inadvertently onto the floor) tickling each other and hiding from the other, then often "fake-argue" over whose turn it is to make breakfast (if it's morning). At night we usually caress each other and talk quietly until we fall asleep, often with my partner still inside me; always holding each other. (woman, 22)

Obviously, what is happening with these people is much more than simply lying together. They are actively engaged in expressing love, warmth, and satisfaction through touch and caress.

Although many people who are less than satisfied with their relationships also mentioned physical contact after intercourse, their descriptions paint a very different picture.

We usually just lie there right after intercourse. Then we hold each other close for a while and talk a little. The talk is usually about work that we have to do for school. (woman, 25)

I want to be touched and told I matter and that the experience was good. I want to touch and gently kiss him, never being physically separated from him. (woman, 23)

I usually pull up the covers to avoid chill after sweating. I've found that men generally prefer to roll over and sleep, not touching, whereas I and women that I've discussed this with prefer to curl up and continue touching/close contact. (woman, 25)

I lie on top of my partner for awhile. Generally do not pull out until I'm limp enough to fall out. (man, 26)

Physical closeness after sex does not necessarily mean emotional closeness. Passive contact may mean fatigue rather than warmth, and if the contact is rough it can be emotionally, if not physically, unpleasant. Mary Gordon described such afterplay in her novel *Final Payments*. The main character, having just had intercourse in a car, describes her partner's caress: "He handled my breast as if he were making a meatball."[4]

Most of the time, however, physical contact implies at least some tendency toward intimacy. If you turn away from your partner right after sex, it is very likely to be taken as avoidance of intimacy. The view of some men on this matter is expressed by Jerry, who, like so many of us, is divorced.

I like to be left alone

Jerry is a 27-year-old accountant who lives in Philadelphia with the children from his recently ended marriage. Also sharing his home now is a 24-year-old woman with whom he has been having a sexual relationship for eight months. They have sex from four to six times a week, and Jerry admits that he would like to do it a little less often.

For Jerry orgasm seems to mean "end." The five minutes after intercourse are not important to him, although he believes them to be as important as orgasm to his partner. Their typical afterplay consists of several minutes of continued body contact, followed by some conversation or reading. Actually, Jerry would like to separate physically from his partner immediately after his orgasm; she is the one eager to stay close.

He puts it this way: "I like to be left alone after intercourse. My body feels strange and I don't like to be fondled." His ideal postcoital experience would be to "lie around and relax and have pleasant conversation and maybe take a nap." What he expressly does not like is "being fawned over after sex."

How very painful the man's desire for separation can be to his partner was brought home to us by a woman in her thirties who has been married for six years. She described her postintercourse experience briefly and poignantly: "What I do—separate, lie silently (usually) without caresses (unless they are specifically requested from me) for about five minutes. No kissing. What I feel—unsatisfied, alone."

Talk

It's the best time to be told you're loved and to say it to someone else. (woman, 40)

Talking is the most distinctively human behavior; and unless you are talking to yourself, it means that you are sharing. Whenever human beings get together someone is likely to be talking. In fact, situations in which people are awake and *not* talking are principally of three types: we are with people we do not know at all (for example, a group of strangers on an elevator); we are with people we know well to whom we feel there is little to say; or we are having sex. It is interesting that at moments of the greatest as well as the least intimacy there is little or no conversation. We may vocalize or verbalize somewhat during intercourse and orgasm, but these sounds would hardly qualify as conversation. Intelligent discourse during orgasm is difficult if not impossible. During sex we join the rest of the animal kingdom, not just in the very basic act of coupling itself, but in the speechlessness that usually accompanies it.

Shortly after sex, most people seem to feel a need to reaffirm their humanness. Talking is an obvious way to do this. After a few minutes, your or your partner's reluctance to talk may be seen as an attempt to escape or even as a sign of hostility.

In Question 44 we asked how often the respondent conversed with his or her partner after sex.

	Percentages	
Response	Men	Women
Never	0	0.7
Infrequently	2.2	2.2

Sometimes	16.7	18.0
About half the time	12.2	7.9
Often	31.1	29.5
Always	37.8	41.7

A high proportion—70 percent—of those we sampled told us that conversation was a frequent or inevitable part of their afterplay; conversation was the most consistently engaged in activity. We discovered from essay answers and the responses to other questions that touching and talking are the most common postcoital behaviors among those who do not go right to sleep. But although talking is a regular activity for many of us after sex, one person in five gave responses ("never," "infrequently," and "sometimes") indicating that for them it is not common.

What is afterplay like for these people? Here is the case of one of them, Barbara L.

Very occasionally we talk

Thirty-one-year-old Barbara L. lives in Hartford, Connecticut, with her optometrist-husband and their two children. They are both athletic and enjoy physical activity. It is, in fact, her husband's physical appearance that most attracts her. They have known each other for nine years and she says that they have never experienced any sexual problems. She has an orgasm every time they have sex.

Sometimes, directly after orgasm, one or both of them want physical separation. When they do stay physically close, it is for about five minutes. They sometimes praise each other after sex, but rarely speak romantically. When asked what she does and how she feels after intercourse, Barbara replies, "Usually I wash after the feeling of relaxation has worn off, and then I read or go to sleep. Very occasionally we talk. I feel very close to my partner for a few minutes—sometimes that feeling lasts through till morning."

Barbara says the postorgasmic period is important for her, but feels it is of no importance to her husband. She "would like to talk and have more body contact after sex—with some romantic talk and maybe some compliments on my femininity, etc." She does not like "the quick separation."

A professional woman in her late thirties, who has been married for ten years, described her postintercourse experience in similar terms: "I am usually wide awake and ready for a good talk with my partner. But since he is usually tired, I end up reading for a while." She described herself as "longing for relaxed talk no matter what the subject may be."

A married man in his early thirties said, "I lie next to my wife for a while. We are usually silent. I feel I have nothing to say, just lying there. Then we read or watch TV."

But most people do have something to say to each other. What is the nature of this talk? For example, how many of us praise our partners after sex or speak romantically? We asked about this in Questions 28 and 30:

HOW OFTEN DO YOU PRAISE YOUR PARTNER AFTER
INTERCOURSE?

	Percentages	
Response	Men	Women
Never or almost never	15.4	10.8
Sometimes	23.1	33.0
About half the time	12.1	13.7
Usually	24.2	23.7
Always or almost always	25.3	18.7

HOW OFTEN DO YOU SPEAK ROMANTICALLY TO YOUR
PARTNER AFTER INTERCOURSE?

	Percentages	
Response	Men	Women
Never or almost never	20.4	14.9
Sometimes	37.6	34.8
About half the time	4.3	6.4
Usually	17.2	25.5
Always or almost always	20.4	18.4

A comparison of these two tables suggests that men are somewhat more likely to praise than they are to speak romantically, whereas for women the two types of statements are roughly equal in frequency. It is also worth noting that other questionnaire responses showed that the woman's orgasmic frequency is unrelated to the frequency with which she either praises her partner or speaks romantically to him.

When these responses are compared to those for Question 44 (how often the respondent converses with his or her partner), it becomes clear that the content of our postsex conversations is not always what we tend to think of as "pillow talk." More than 50 percent of our sample praise or speak romantically to their partners half the time or less. This is true for both men and women. About one man in five never, or hardly ever, speaks romantically after lovemaking, and among women the percentage is only slightly lower. Generally those who do not speak romantically tend not to praise either. If the intercourse and orgasm are positive experiences, is it necessary to have intimate verbal contact afterward? Do people really like tender conversation and talk of love and romance at this time? We will see in later chapters that although people might not *ask* for postcoital verbal intimacy, it is often very much desired. In fact the absence of reinforcing comments after sex may be quite detrimental to a relationship.

In their answers to the question of what they did after sex, 90 respondents specifically mentioned talking. But of course there are all kinds of talk. Considering the clear significance of verbal communication, some people's postcoital conversation is so inappropriate that they would be better off silent.

For some reason, after sex my wife and I occasionally end up arguing. She often brings up certain problems we are having. (man, 38)

Obviously between romantic talk and argument there is a wide range of conversational possibilities. For some people, not surprisingly, the sexual encounter itself is the main topic of conversation.

We talk of our lovemaking experience—praising the other and/or sharing our sexual highs and lows (likes and dislikes). (woman, 25)

For 5–10 minutes after intercourse, we hold each other and talk about how we feel and did feel during intercourse. (woman, 23)

We'll just lie quietly or murmur our satisfaction, comment on particularly delightful parts of the intercourse—exchange any apologies or explanations if one wasn't feeling adequate. (woman, 26)

In some cases, giving and receiving assurance for my performance and his. (woman, 22)

May talk about any number of things. Sometimes talk about what we liked or disliked about the recent intercourse. (woman, 23)

And for some, these discussions are especially important. A man in his mid-20s, living with a woman a little older than he, said:

If I stay in bed I usually hold or stroke my partner and we talk for a while—about our lovemaking or other shared experience. I feel that talking about intercourse has rewards that are at least as great as the act itself, with tangible benefits to both partners. The difficulty is breaking the taboo that exists; We don't talk about sex often enough. Talking about sex is like the act itself—once you start doing it, you don't want to stop.

It may appear on the surface that there is nothing wrong with such discussions of likes and dislikes, highs and lows, etc. But consider this: If people commented on or evaluated their foreplay experience and behavior while having intercourse, a lot of pleasure would be killed by conversation. Similarly, if you discuss the other aspects of the sexual encounter at length during afterplay, you may be missing out on its own pleasures. Even worse, depending on the kinds of things you have to say about other aspects of the sexual encounter, you may turn the whole thing into a disaster. We will discuss such disasters in Chapter 6.

For now, the following case history and quotes that follow show how conversation in the postcoital period can be significant—and positive.

A time to talk

Dave, a researcher at a large hospital in San Francisco, met his wife when he was 21. Now 33, he has been married for ten years and has three children. He is very pleased with the way his marriage has turned out and he believes his wife to be as happy with it as he is.

Although Dave would like to have sex somewhat more often than he does, which is less than once a week, he says he is satisfied with his sexual relationship. He also enjoys the time after sex, as does his wife. Neither of them falls asleep immediately, nor does either of them prefer to be physically separated from the other. For Dave this is a time to "sit and talk" and perhaps have a glass of wine. He feels "warm, loving, comfortable, and happy."

He likes the atmosphere for afterplay to be a comfortable one, "a time when one can be intimate in a conversational or intellectual way—a time to talk about the things I or my partner think about but don't normally convey to other people—one's life, goals, problems, desires, etc."

When asked about potentially unpleasant afterplay experiences, he describes only one, "that in which my partner would become cold or withdrawn, unwilling to communicate."

Although Dave considers orgasm to be the most important part of a sexual encounter, and imagines that his wife attaches to it the same importance, he feels that the five minutes after intercourse are nearly as important as orgasm, and equal in importance to foreplay and intercourse itself.

Other respondents also expressed positive feelings about after-sex conversation:

A dreamy, relaxed time which is conducive to very free talk. Things can be discussed that cannot be approached at other times. (woman, 34)

We often talk about our children after sex, about the cute things they did or said; not about the problems. (man, 32)

Our most honest and risk-taking conversations have been after intercourse. (woman, 22)

I hug and caress my partner and engage in some conversation, telling my partner how good I feel when close to her. (man, 27)

When conversation is positive and personal, words spoken after sex can enhance a relationship. Certainly this is true for a 25-year-old professional woman, who has been married for four years, who reported that after intercourse she holds her husband very close, kisses him, and praises him about "how great he is and how much I love him."

Get Clean, Dry, and Comfortable

How many people always wash up after intercourse? Are there people who never do? Washing up was one of the activities we asked about in Question 44. Here are the responses:

	Percentages	
Response	Men	Women
Never	12.4	12.9
Infrequently	14.6	15.8
Sometimes	23.6	26.6
About half the time	9.0	12.2
Often	21.3	13.7
Always	19.1	18.7

Looking at these percentages, we can see that men are somewhat more likely than women to wash up within the hour after intercourse. We can also see that there is plenty of variability. Although 40 percent of men and more than 30 percent of women say they usually or always wash, more than a quarter of both sexes say they rarely if ever do.

In response to Question 40, in which respondents were asked to describe what they did right after intercourse, 24 people mentioned washing up or drying off.

If we don't fall asleep right after, we usually go into the shower together. (woman, 29)

Directly after, my partner and I usually kiss and hold each other;

one of us then usually goes for a towel—or we'll shower. (woman, 26)

We usually get some tissues and wipe up the semen, etc. Then we lie close to each other until we fall asleep, usually in the nude. (man, 39)

. . . Eventually get up and take a joint shower. (man, 28)

After "an appropriate time" (sometime after full flaccidity but not long after, 2–10 minutes I suspect), I "de-vaginate" and go to dry off with a towel. Sometimes I bring a towel to my partner. (man, 52)

Clean-up (briefly—no douching!) (woman, 25)

As soon as orgasm is over and he loses the erection, we like to pull away momentarily to wipe ourselves with paper towels and generally get "non-sticky" and dry. (woman, 26)

Do the "get up and get a towel" routine, clean ourselves off. . . . Sometimes we rub each other with the towel in a very tender ritual. (man, 32)

The reference, in the final quote, to the "get up and get a towel routine" confirms that people often assume they are doing what everyone or almost everyone is also doing after sex. But the fact is that for a large percentage of couples getting up and getting a towel is not only not routine, it is not even occasional. In fact, for some people staying in bed exactly "as is" is enjoyable in itself. There is nothing inherently good or bad about washing up or drying off after sex, except for its effect on your partner. The key question is this: Whatever you do, do you do it together? Do you shower while your partner is toweling off in bed? Do you immediately brush your teeth, gargle, and generally scrub clean while your partner wonders where you've gone?

We shall see in Chapter 5 that washing and bathing *together* can be a sensual and especially pleasant afterplay experience.

Yet if you rush out of bed to clean up you may be leaving behind a formerly satisfied but now angry or troubled partner.

Another activity on our list was going to the bathroom. (We could have been more specific, but we felt that to do so would have broken the mood of the questionnaire.)

	Percentages	
Response	Men	Women
Never	6.7	4.3
Infrequently	17.8	9.4
Sometimes	28.9	31.7
About half the time	17.8	13.7
Often	18.9	20.1
Always	10.0	20.9

Again, these percentages show plenty of variability. But in this case, women are somewhat more likely than men to go to the bathroom after sex. One possible reason is that many women may want to release the semen from the vagina, which is done conveniently in the bathroom (such release is automatic when the woman urinates).

Although going to the bathroom is clearly common among postcoital behaviors, it was specifically mentioned by only four people in the essay question. For the healthy human being, few activities are less memorable than the typical trip to the bathroom. Yet this is the sum and substance of afterplay for some people.

Listen to Music

For about 30 percent of those we surveyed, listening to music was a frequent part of afterplay, and music is often on before and during intercourse as well. (Making music is a literal form of afterplay for one male respondent, who said he liked to play the guitar in bed after sex.) When asked how often they listened to music during the hour after intercourse, people said:

| | Percentages | |
Response	Men	Women
Never	14.6	11.6
Infrequently	23.6	16.7
Sometimes	23.6	29.0
About half the time	7.9	10.1
Often	21.3	23.9
Always	9.0	8.7

Only two people specifically mentioned music in the essay responses (one was a teen-age girl, the other a man in his twenties who said he listened to jazz on occasion). What accounts for this discrepancy? It could be that for some people music is such an ever-present part of their lives that they are unlikely to notice it as part of the postintercourse period. This would be unfortunate, if true, because music, as we shall see, can be a highly enjoyable element in afterplay.

Have More Sex

Sometimes, of course, afterplay becomes foreplay:

After making love for the first time, I usually perform oral sex on my partner to arouse him again. I usually do have intercourse more than once a night. (woman, 30)

How often do the people in our sample have sex more than once in a typical lovemaking session?

Response	Percentages	
	Men	Women
Never	16.1	11.6
Infrequently	21.8	26.1
Sometimes	39.1	34.8
About half the time	8.0	9.4
Often	13.8	14.5
Always	1.1	3.6

Not surprisingly, we found age to be a major correlate with the frequency of multiple intercourse sessions—on the average, the older we are the less likely it is that our afterplay will lead to more sex. As is well known, the male's refractory period—the period following orgasm in which sexual stimulation is to no avail—steadily lengthens as he gets older. This means that in order to have sex again, the couple needs a sufficient amount of time. Since many of us devote very little time to afterplay, it is not surprising that we don't have time for more sex. This problem with time is perhaps best shown by the following response from a 25-year-old single man who has been regularly seeing a woman for a year:

Talk, caress my partner, listen to my radio and have more sex (providing there is time. There never seems enuf.) We do a lot of quickies simply 'cuz we are so busy.

He was even too busy to write out all the letters in "enough" and "because."
Some other comments:

I may often want to engage in actual intercourse and achieve orgasm, but am tired and feel it would take too much time or energy. (woman, 26)

Usually there is a period of caressing and just generally basking in the postorgasmic euphoria. This lasts for about twenty minutes. Sometimes after that period if time permits we'll resume foreplay and before you know it we're basking in postorgasmic euphoria once again. (man, 30)

If we don't fall asleep or don't have to go anywhere after intercourse, I feel like starting all over again. (woman, 25)

As is the case with other afterplay activities, whether having sex more than once is a thing to be avoided or sought after depends entirely on the people and circumstances. We do feel, however, that it should not be considered the ultimate in afterplay experiences. We have found no correlation between how happy a person is with his or her overall relationship and how often he or she engages in more than one session of intercourse.

For some of us additional sex means that we are unable to experience the many other joys and intimacies of the postcoital period. By the time we have finished with subsequent intercourse, we are too tired to enjoy any other kind of afterplay. We see this in the following case:

Nothing better than sex

Jennifer is an art student in New York City. She is 17 years old and has been living with a 24-year-old man for the past seven months. Jennifer feels good about this relationship and she very much enjoys their sexual activities. She would like to have intercourse "much more often," but there aren't enough hours in the day. She and her boyfriend have sex about 15 times a week—often two or three times in an evening—and she says she has four orgasms during a typical love-making session. It is not communication or intimacy that Jennifer feels is most important about sex. For Jennifer "there is nothing better than sex to relieve tense emotions."

After intercourse Jennifer notes that "First we get a towel, then we just lie in bed and relax. Sometimes we talk and listen to music." Although Jennifer would like her boyfriend to lie next to her, hugging and caressing her for a while, he is almost always exhausted and goes right to sleep.

We certainly do not mean to suggest that more sex always means less of other kinds of closeness. For many people additional sex is an expression of love.

Most of the time I'm enthusiastic about repeating the wonderful loving experience; if our physical resources are capable, we'll make love again. (woman, 27)

Eat and Drink

> Tis not the meat, but 'tis the appetite
> Makes eating a delight.
> —John Suckling (1609–1642)

When one's "sexual appetite" has been somewhat sated, another major appetite may take its place. For some people food never tastes better than it does after sex. But the percentage of men and women who regularly eat in the postintercourse period is not high:

	Percentages	
Response	*Men*	*Women*
Never	23.9	26.1
Infrequently	36.4	26.8
Sometimes	21.6	31.2
About half the time	10.2	5.1
Often	6.8	8.0
Always	1.1	2.9

This evidence that eating is not common afterplay is supported by the fact that only 11 people specifically mentioned it in the essay question about what things they do after sex. Women, more often than men, mentioned eating in the essay question, and the responses to Question 44 show a very slight tendency for women to eat after sex more often than men. It is interesting to note that one of the few articles we have seen addressed specifically to the postintercourse experience was devoted entirely to the joys of postcoital pasta.[5] Also, eating with one's lover was mentioned by several of our respondents in their descriptions of highly desirable afterplay. We suspect that eating would be more common were it not so late and lovers so tired.

What about drinking?
Previous research[6] has shown that a large number of people at least occasionally have an alcoholic drink *prior* to intercourse, but what about after? What proportion of women, and of men, have a drink then?

	Percentages	
Response	Men	Women
Never	59.1	48.6
Infrequently	14.8	23.9
Sometimes	13.6	19.6
About half the time	6.8	3.6
Often	5.7	2.9
Always	0	1.4

It appears that drinking before sex is far more common than drinking after. Few people mentioned drinking in their description of postintercourse behavior. Among those who did, the drink seemed to serve different purposes for different people. For one respondent, a 33-year-old man who has been married for ten years, "a glass of wine" accompanied sitting and talking with his partner, and he felt "warm, loving, comfortable, and happy." But a 30-year-old single woman said she sometimes felt "nervous anxiety which will get me up out of bed and drive me to drink alcohol . . . or leave altogether."

Alcohol serves many functions, one of which is to reduce anxiety. This may be one of the reasons it is widely used before sex, when performance anxiety may be a problem. After intercourse there is usually much less anxiety and tension, which makes the need for alcohol less likely. But this is a time when food or drink can be shared and savored. In Chapter 5 we will see that there are varieties of food and drink that people find particularly desirable during afterplay.

Smoke

One of the important social changes occurring in the United States today is the change in attitudes toward cigarette smoking. For the first time nonsmokers are asserting themselves both verbally and legally.

Has this change been reflected in postcoital smoking habits? There is no way to be certain, since we have no prior data for comparison. In movies, cartoons, and books we still come across the stereotype of one or both partners reaching for a postcoital cigarette; in fact, a prominent attorney suggested to us that the cover of this book show a hand reaching for a cigarette.

There is thus some reason to believe that, at least a few years ago, smoking after sex was rather common. But for the men and women we surveyed, smoking is not a common part of afterplay. We asked how often the respondent smoked a cigarette in the hour after intercourse:

	Percentages	
Response	Men	Women
Never	69.3	64.7
Infrequently	6.8	7.2
Sometimes	6.8	8.6
About half the time	4.5	2.9
Often	3.4	7.2
Always	9.1	9.4

For 80 percent of our sample, smoking is, at most, an occasional activity.

Eight people listed smoking as one of their postcoital behaviors. And the word "listed" is quite appropriate here. There was a tendency for those who did smoke literally to *list* their activities and feelings. For example, a 45-year-old man wrote:

Hunt for a towel
Smoke a cigarette
Get a drink
Speak softly about love
Watch TV
Go to sleep

And a 36-year-old woman wrote:

Feel smug
Feel mellow
Smoke a cigarette
Talk
Touch

If very few people smoke during foreplay and intercourse, why do some people smoke during afterplay? Probably the most basic reason for smoking is that nicotine is physiologically addicting. For people who smoke regularly, time spent in foreplay and intercourse leaves them in a state of nicotine withdrawal—and likely to begin their afterplay with a cigarette. Of course people can do other things while they smoke, but smoking does limit postcoital possibilities. Very basic and important activities such as kissing, hugging, or cuddling are difficult if not dangerous while smoking. And smoking can often be a routinized, almost unconscious habit, undermining the awareness that should characterize afterplay.

Another type of smoking was mentioned by several persons: marijuana. Only a few of our respondents said they smoke marijuana after sex, but it is possible that more people would have listed it in their essays were it not for the continued illegality of the drug.

The one variable that has an undeniable effect on the desirability or undesirability of smoking anything during afterplay is how your partner feels about it. As we shall see in Chapter 6, a number of people have very definite reactions to their partner's postcoital cigarettes.

Watch Television or Read

I'm satisfied with my postintercourse experience except when there's a guest host on the Tonight Show. (man, 27)

Some late night television programming may reflect the network's knowledge that for many people the program they watch is a component of their afterplay. One reason for the 15-year survival of Johnny Carson's *Tonight Show* may well be that Carson's style is better suited to the postintercourse period than that of his rivals.

Here are the responses to Question 44 as to how often people watch TV in the hour following sex:

	Percentages	
Response	Men	Women
Never	36.4	32.4
Infrequently	22.7	28.8
Sometimes	27.3	24.5
About half the time	9.1	6.5
Often	2.3	7.9
Always	2.3	0

For nearly 15 percent of the people we sampled, television is a common postintercourse activity. Also, the percentage of people who say they never watch television after sex is considerably lower than the percentage who say they never smoke or drink.

We will see that watching television is more likely to be considered a negative rather than a desirable postintercourse activity, especially when the TV is turned on within minutes after lovemaking. Watching TV can often signify going back to relatively isolated, separate routines. And no matter how much you like Johnny Carson, you cannot hold him.

What about reading after sex? Our respondents did not give it high marks as a postcoital activity. Only one included it in the ideal, whereas five people included it among things they particularly did not or would not like their partners to do after sex. The reason for this, we suspect, is that reading is ordinarily not a shared activity. It can be shared, however, One man in his late thirties reported that he and his partner derive great pleasure from reading to each other after making love.

How many people curl up with a good (or not so good) book before, after, or instead of curling up with their partner in the postintercourse period? Here are the percentages in Question 44 for reading after sex:

	Percentages	
Response	Men	Women
Never	49.4	44.9
Infrequently	22.5	31.9
Sometimes	16.9	15.9
About half the time	5.6	2.2
Often	4.5	4.3
Always	1.1	0.7

Reading, it would seem, is often a substitute for what is much more strongly desired: touching and talking.

Work

First you work, then you play.
—Grandma's Rule (cited in *Parents Are Teachers* by Wesley Becker)

How often do people reverse Grandma's Rule and have sex just before working?

	Percentages	
Response	Men	Women
Never	32.2	34.8
Infrequently	35.6	24.6
Sometimes	28.7	32.6
About half the time	1.1	6.5
Often	2.3	0.7
Always	0	0.7

The percentage profiles for work are similar to those for television watching (probably the major American nonwork activity), except that fewer people, especially males, have sex before work with any degree of regularity—less than four percent of the men and less than eight percent of the women.

Since most of us work in the daytime (we are including unpaid housework as work), another way of considering the above data is as a reflection of how many people typically have sex in the morning or afternoon. We asked this question directly in the questionnaire and found that only five percent of the men and ten percent of the women said the morning was their most common time for sex; for afternoon lovemaking the percentages are five and eight percent, respectively.

In their essay answers, a number of people specifically mentioned going to work or beginning the day's activity. Their responses generally indicated that sex in the daylight hours provided a little relaxation prior to or in the midst of the day's responsibilities:

I get up and go about my day. I feel somewhat more relaxed. (man, 41)

Since usually I have intercourse in the A.M., I usually get up within 5–10 minutes and go about the day's activity. (woman, 32)

At first I relax and enjoy the recently enjoyed pleasure. Alas, within minutes I must usually get up and tend to the basic necessities and realities of life—i.e., one 18-month-old who is waking from his nap, making lunch, showering, and getting ready to go out. (woman, 32)

We usually hold each other 5–10 minutes—if it's night we usually sleep within the half hour. Often we have intercourse after his seven-year-old son leaves for school, after which we usually clean up and he goes to work within the half hour (we still lie quietly for 10 minutes or so before getting up). (woman, 24)

Some people's schedules permit longer lovemaking sessions in which there can be much intimate afterplay before either or both return to work. In these cases the afterplay experience is clearly more positive. A man in his 40s reported that he would occasionally leave his office for a "lunch break" lasting several hours:

We lie around talking about ourselves, relishing our time together. It's incredible how easy it is to forget about work in this kind of atmosphere. My clients and business associates probably wonder why I'm sometimes in such a good mood late in the day.

Other Postintercourse Behaviors

In the space for "Other" in Question 44 and in the essay responses, interviews, and so on, we were told of other postcoital activities, ones which could not easily be classified. We list them here, without making any kind of value judgments. But as you will see, some of these are close to what people describe in ideal afterplay and some are similar to activities described as negative.

If you do any of the following after sex, you have company:

Nurse the baby
Bake bread
Go to the movies
Ride horseback
Walk the dog
Play cards or monopoly
Move around to cool off
Smile
Cry
Play backgammon
Watch pornographic films
Fantasize

Socialize
Sew
Write
Use dental floss
Figure out what I'll tell my wife
Look at my partner
Masturbate
Improvise songs
Oh-oh-oh-oh (the entire response to Question 40 from a 21-year-old woman)

And if you are a woman, and the first thing you do after sex is to "cough and/or push the penis out," you too are not alone.

Conclusions

So what are your neighbors doing after they "do it"? Based on our study, in a typical hour after sex:

80 percent of us talk, 50 percent of us praise our partners and/or speak romantically.

76 percent continue some kind of physical contact, but often for only a few minutes. Also, for many the contact is passive.

67 percent sleep; more than 33 percent of us do so within minutes (sleep is, as expected, more common among men).

50 percent go to the bathroom.

48 percent wash up.

38 percent listen to music.

23 percent have sex again.

17 percent smoke a cigarette.

15 percent have something to eat.

14 percent watch television.

10 percent have a drink.

9 percent read.

5 percent work.

Keep in mind that the above figures are for typical activities, defined as those in which one or both partners engage at least half the time. If the occasional participants are included, the percentages go much higher. For example, over 60 percent of us will from time to time turn on the TV after sex, and 75 percent of us eat something at least once in a while.

What does all this tell us about the state of American afterplay? Picture ten couples, randomly selected. Five of them don't exchange loving words after supposedly *making* love, and in two couples hardly any words are exchanged at all. Two or three couples remain in physical contact only long enough to detach from one another, and someone is asleep within minutes in at least three of the couples.

Afterplay presents the opportunity for a variety of pleasurable activities, and yet so many of us do so little. So what? There are lots of things we could eat for breakfast, too, but most of us stick with coffee, toast, bacon and eggs, or cereal.

Breakfast is, emotionally speaking, a rather subdued time. Some of us are barely functioning at all as we eat it. The small range of foods is accompanied by a small range of moods. We may be grumpy or we may be feeling pretty good and ready to meet the day. But as we shall see in the next chapter, the range of emotions in afterplay is great—and these emotions are often intense. People used words like "alone," "despondent," or "joyful" to describe how they felt after lovemaking. We doubt that your breakfast would be likely to give you such feelings. Despondency and aloneness are the kinds of things of which divorces are made. More so, we are convinced, than burnt toast.

Afterplay, to put it quite simply, offers the possibility of joy. As one woman in her mid-40s reported:

Very often I will experience intercourse and orgasm just so we can get into those special postintercourse feelings and moods.

CHAPTER 4

How People Feel

Everyone knows how important feelings and emotions are, and yet psychologists know little about them. Paul T. Young, a psychologist himself, wrote, "Almost everyone except the psychologist knows what an emotion is."[1] Emotions, being personal and private, are difficult to study scientifically. We just cannot see the emotions of other people directly.

Everyday language paints a particular picture of feelings. Many times they are referred to as uncontrollable ("I don't know why, I feel so anxious today;" "For some reason I feel great")— or as causing behaviors ("I laughed because I was happy;" "I cried because I was sad"). Although the reasons we feel the way we do are often so obscure as to be nearly impossible to locate, the reasons for our emotions are sometimes obvious. And though the way we feel certainly influences the way we behave, the reverse may also be true: What you do or don't do in the postintercourse period may have a considerable effect on how you feel and how your partner feels about it and about you.

We need not belabor the obvious fact that feelings are important, that those events that evoke our strongest emotions are often the most significant events in our lives. The very big ones—the births, the deaths—come infrequently for most of us, but there is another event the emotional intensity of which rivals that of life's comings and goings: the sexual encounter. Since our bodies are intimately involved in our emotions (we simply cannot be excited if our hearts are not racing), it is not surprising that sexual activity would lead to intense emotionality.

In the postintercourse period our emotions do seem to be closer to the surface. As one woman said, "The emotional impact is greater at this time. I feel more vulnerable." Vulnerability should not be confused with weakness; our respondents seem to imply that being open to your own and your partner's feelings is often quite positive. Another respondent said, "I feel intensely vulnerable; if the relationship is going well, I feel strength in the sharing of vulnerability."

One reason why feelings seem to be so central in afterplay is that at this time people are more aware than usual of their bodies—which, as always, are fueling their emotions. As one respondent put it, "After reaching orgasm I feel terrific and quite content to just feel the effects of lovemaking in my body. Usually my lover's body is tingling and quite warm."

In the following case, Robert W. recognizes that he is vulnerable and open in the postcoital period. He appreciates the sensitivity his wife has always provided in afterplay.

Her eyes still sparkle

Robert W. married his childhood sweetheart when he was 19, and they have been together for 32 years. He is a pharmacist in Boston, where he and his wife have raised seven children, two of whom no longer live at home.

Robert stays in shape by jogging and playing sports with his family. He rarely watches television and prefers to spend his spare time with his family and friends. Robert is a sensitive man who really enjoys expressing his gratitude when someone does him a favor or has been good to him.

Robert and his wife have sex about three times a week, and he always has an orgasm. It wasn't always this way. In the early years of their relationship, he occasionally had difficulties. But he always felt that his wife understood—and, he notes, whatever problems he did have were never magnified by her. Robert very much enjoys the postintercourse time with his wife, during which they almost always compliment each other or speak affectionately. "I like to hold my wife, sometimes kiss her and nuzzle her cheeks," he says. After sex he feels "very relaxed and needed, comfortable and satisfied." He finds their ". . . bedroom to be very pleasant," and he "wouldn't care to be anywhere else. My wife expresses her pleasure by cuddling me and occasionally expresses verbally and briefly that she has enjoyed our sex. This pleases me and I do not desire anything different."

Robert has never had a negative postintercourse experience and for this he credits his wife. "I can imagine that if she should dismiss me by turning away abruptly, it would hurt. I cannot even imagine my wife expressing a negative reaction. She is much too sensitive to my needs to hurt me. Although I'm sure she knows she could hurt me, I am equally sure she would not."

Robert obviously appreciates—and returns—his wife's love and understanding: "She is a miraculous mother and grandmother. At nearly half a century old her eyes still sparkle and she has a sexy mouth. But most of all, she is honest. I realize again what a really lucky guy I am."

Robert seems "lucky" in another sense: he's neither afraid nor mistrustful of his emotions. Many people are. Among them are those who equate emotionality with confusion and rationality with clarity, believing that if we could rely primarily on reason rather than emotion we could find truths and eliminate conflict. But "purely" rational thought does not, of course, banish differences between people—nor is it likely to help us establish objective truths. In fact it may be that all of our logical arguments, reasoning, and actions are merely mustered to support our emotions: When we feel something we find reasons for our convictions.

Which is why any account of sexuality limited to our thoughts and actions simply will not do. Our personal and private feelings are the most real and complete phenomena we can experience. William James suggests[2] that the importance of the personal and private, the "subjective" side of things, cannot be overestimated:

> The axis of reality runs solely through the egoistic places— they are strung upon it like so many beads. To describe the world with all the various feelings of the individual pinch of destiny . . . left out from the description—they being as describable as anything else—would be something like offering a printed bill of fare as the equivalent for a solid meal . . . a bill of fare with one real raisin on it instead of the word "raisin," with one real egg instead of the word "egg" might be an inadequate meal, but it would at least be a commencement of reality.

In order to obtain the individual feelings—the real eggs and raisins—we asked people to describe how they feel right after intercourse and over the next half hour or so. We did not follow the usual practice of providing a checklist of possible feelings— we did not want a respondent to check off "content" when what he or she really meant was "vulnerable, and impervious to the pressures of the world."

Let's take a look at these verbal descriptions of postcoital feelings. The range of the feelings is enormous, from negative ones—frustration, loneliness, guilt, and exhaustion—through the positive feelings of relaxation, energy, and satisfaction, to the strongly positive experiences of warmth, love, and transcendence. If your own postcoital feelings are more negative than positive, do not despair. There are many other people who feel the way you do, and, more important, feelings can change.

Frustrated

Frustration experienced as a result of not having an orgasm is definitely related to gender. All of the eight people from our sample who mentioned frustration as a postcoital feeling are women. This is hardly surprising, since 94 percent of male respondents but only 44 percent of female respondents reported having an orgasm more than 90 percent of the time. But frustration is by no means an inevitable result of not having an orgasm: the vast majority of women who reach orgasm at least half the time did *not* say they experienced any frustration or disappointment when they did not have one. These feelings appear to be common and important only to women for whom orgasm is infrequent or nonexistent.

Thus, when failure to experience orgasm is not a regular occurrence, most women are still able to enjoy closeness, warmth, and intimate contact. On the other hand, women who usually do not reach orgasm may find that physical closeness makes their problem worse:

I feel close to my partner except on frustrating occasions, in which case I don't want to have further body contact as it is more frustrating. (woman, 23)

For some women who are frustrated, feelings of anger and resentment are the direct consequence:

My feelings depend on the act. If complete and fulfilling, I usually fall asleep within a half-hour. If not, it's the usual feelings of frustration and anger and no one to scream at without causing even more frustration and anger. (woman, 46)

I usually feel warm after intercourse especially if we both orgasmed. If we haven't (meaning I haven't) I feel resentful. (woman, 25)

When I fail to have an orgasm with someone I don't love, I am irritated after sex. I feel aggressive and hostile. At these times I initiate wrestling as a way in which to relieve myself. (woman, 21)

Aggression is but one accompaniment to sexual frustration. Some people feel disappointed or tense. Some masturbate:

I just feel disappointed and frustrated because of my inability to reach orgasm. (woman, 27)

For 5–10 minutes after intercourse, we hold each other and talk about how we feel and did feel during intercourse. After a few minutes we'll take turns in the bathroom and then sleep in separate beds for the rest of the night. I usually feel disappointed that I have not had an orgasm, but I have enjoyed the time of physical intimacy. It's very difficult for me to relax enough to go to sleep afterward. (woman, 23)

Sometimes I feel frustrated and I masturbate. (woman, 23)

Orgasmic dysfunction in women was once thought to be immune to treatment. In the third edition of a widely used textbook in abnormal psychology, published in 1964, James C. Coleman wrote that "it may be extremely difficult or impossible" to modify what was then called "frigidity." Feelings of frustration were thought to be part of the burden of being a woman. In the 1970s the situation has changed dramatically, and in the fifth edition of his book—published in 1976—Coleman is rightfully more optimistic: "With competent treatment, some 60 to 100 percent of sexual dysfunction (including orgasmic dysfunction) can be treated successfully."[3] William Masters and Virginia Johnson have shown, in *Human Sexual Inadequacy*, that in a two-week program, therapy was successful in over 80 percent of the cases treated.[4] There are more and better-trained sex therapists available today than ever before. And there are good self-help books too, such as *Becoming Orgasmic: A Sexual Growth Program for Women* by Julia Heiman, Leslie LoPiccolo, and Joseph LoPiccolo. The prognosis for orgasmic dysfunction in women—and incidentally, its companion problem, premature ejaculation—looks good indeed.

Also, improved communications between the sexes should prove helpful. As women become more assertive it seems likely that we will see fewer reports like the following from a 19-year-old woman:

I always feel pretty disappointed because I usually was not assertive enough so neither my partner nor I got what we wanted. For this reason most of the time I feel frustrated and tense, both emotionally and physically.

Fortunately, increasing numbers of women feel more comfortable in showing their partners what they find pleasurable, especially with respect to genital stimulation.

Feelings of frustration are not nearly as common nor as painful as some other negative feelings in the postcoital period. Although it may be unpleasant to have the need for orgasm unsatisfied, we have found from our respondents that there are more important needs. If *these* needs are not filled in the postintercourse period, the effects can be even more frustrating. One woman said, "Feeling the closeness of sex and orgasm only to feel cold-shouldered is frustrating indeed." But the cold shoulder can lead to far more painful experiences.

Alone

Of the unpleasant postcoital feelings people may experience that are independent of attaining orgasm, none is more negative than isolation. We may feel great relief and pleasure in orgasm, but orgasm is possible without a partner. And for some couples, the sexual experience amounts to nothing more than mutual masturbation. Although they are in each other's physical presence there is really no contact. This lack of contact is most apparent—and most painful—in the postcoital period. The excitement of foreplay and intercourse, and the intense but brief pleasure of orgasm, may distract one from a feeling of aloneness; but if no real contact has taken place, the heightened vulnerability of the postcoital period brings back even stronger feelings of discomfort, isolation, and despair.

This is the predominant reason why sex without intimacy can be debilitating. We *need* to feel bonds and connections with other people. We *need* contact, intimacy, acceptance, nurturing, and love. We are social animals and we have uniquely human social needs. These needs, more basic than orgasmic needs, can be fulfilled in the postintercourse period. If they are not, we are painfully aware of it. We experience isolation, alienation, aloneness:

What we do is to lie separately and silently. We never touch or caress. I feel dissatisfied and alone. (woman, 38)

I wash up and then go to sleep feeling tremendously let down. It's as if the sex act was an isolated event and now it's back to business as usual. (woman, 33)

I lie awake feeling frustrated because I don't feel close to my partner. I am beginning to resist having sex at all because I don't feel I am a part of it. So I just lie awake thinking about this. (woman, 24)

The following case is of a woman who is highly orgasmic but unhappy.

Sometimes I cry

Dorothy B. is an attractive 37-year-old professional woman who lives with her husband of 11 years in a small suburb outside of Los Angeles. Her physical appearance has always been important to her. Dorothy plays tennis and exercises regularly; she also spends a great deal of time writing, painting, and listening to music. She has several close friends and she values these intimate relationships. Dorothy loves her husband's gentleness and strength, and feels that she has a very good marriage. However, she is concerned because they do not make love as often as they used to. When they do, about once a week, she always reaches a climax.

Dorothy reports that their postcoital closeness "seems to have diminished with the years rather than increased. Earlier in the relationship there was a prolonged period of closeness and sharing after intercourse, but this has lessened." Dorothy would still like her husband to hold her all night. ". . . to hold me and tell me how beautiful it was making love, or hear something wonderful that he thought or felt about me. I would like to share my thoughts and feelings with him. If something special happened during the day I would like to tell him about it and have him do the same."

The intimate sharing of thoughts and feelings in the postcoital period is obviously important to Dorothy. However, there is little of this in their present relationship. What actually happens is best expressed by her:

"I stay in bed and try to talk to my husband about how I feel and how he feels. This is not usually too successful. I want to be held and given assurances. I feel vulnerable, very open to pain or pleasure. I sometimes feel cold when he seems insensitive. Although I feel loving and affectionate, happy and relaxed, these feelings are often ignored by my husband. Then, sometimes, I cry or want to cry even though the intercourse was good."

Although Dorothy often praises her husband and speaks romantically to him after they make love, he never reciprocates. Recently, Dorothy has begun to explore her sexuality in relationships outside her marriage.

Feelings of estrangement are not sick, they are not neurotic. They are simply an indication that something is wrong. Just as physical pain tells us that a part of the body requires attention, psychological and emotional pain tell us that our souls need attention. We need tenderness, affection, closeness, and communication in the postcoital period. If we feel alone, certain behaviors and attitudes can be changed in order to change these feelings—in order to satisfy our postcoital needs.

Some people are willing to be treated badly. They seem to feel that their needs aren't important. If you are among them, if you are willing to be used or exploited sexually or any other way, you probably will be. In fact, this is what feeling used is all about: when the sexual encounter is a release and nothing more, when there is no postcoital warmth, affection, and attention. This is not a typical case of exploitation, since when one person feels used it follows that the partner's critical human needs are also not being fulfilled. No one emerges really happy:

I remember times with earlier partners when I felt absolutely awful—kind of used and simultaneously using. At such points I usually became resentful of the experience and wanted to disassociate myself from it as quickly as possible. (man, 24)

I usually want more affection than I get and I feel somewhat dissatisfied and used. (woman, 21)

Sometimes I want to punch him in the face, but I never do, so I just lie there feeling cheated, used, and incredibly lonely. (woman, 21)

The experience of resignation is characteristic of the attitude of some people who are willing to settle for poor afterplay and poor relationships. As a 31-year-old woman said, "I usually wish it could have been better, but realize that it could have been worse. I usually fall asleep afterwards."

Everyone feels alone from time to time. For no matter how sympathetic or understanding people are, there is always a real physical separation between you and everyone else. When, however, the feeling of aloneness is the emotion most sharply experienced after lovemaking, something is amiss. If it is, you need not be resigned nor resentful. Changing the quality of your afterplay can change the situation for the better.

Guilty

Depth psychologists—Freud and the psychoanalysts—stress the ways in which we seem to be in conflict with ourselves. When we feel guilty, it is because we are at war with ourselves. It is as though a part of us, a feeling or a thought, is sharply disapproving of another feeling or thought. Such conflicts often involve our sexual lives, especially when extramarital affairs are involved. We may feel attracted to someone, want to have sex with him or her, and yet there is a part of us which condemns this desire. If a sexual encounter takes place there may be a momentary satisfaction of the sexual need—along with a corresponding increase in the forces of self-condemnation. Guilt is, after all, the way we punish ourselves.

In our affair the only problem is the tension that is created because we are sometimes pressed for time and it creates anxiety and tension between each other. I sometimes feel a bit guilty. Time is very important to us. (man, 38)

For some reason it is usually at this time that I feel bad about cheating on my husband, and a little paranoid that we might be discovered. (woman, 27)

In these quotes the respondents are consciously acknowledging that there is something not totally right about the extramarital affairs. Their afterplay is then tinged with some fear and anxiety. These people are aware not only of their feelings but of their causes. They are afraid of getting caught by a spouse or hurting their mates, or they feel guilt from the lying and deceiving that goes with "cheating."

In a marital or other regular relationship, the voices of self-recrimination are usually not conscious. We may not feel very good after sex, and not know why. We are not aware of the fact that we are punishing ourselves. But we do indeed feel the effects of this unconscious punishment. We have less obvious and vague feelings of discontent and malaise brought on by our lack of self-acceptance. These too are the effects of guilt. Such feelings may or may not affect sexual functioning itself, but they are very likely to surface during the postcoital period.

Since these feelings are not limited to situations involving extramarital sex, why do we have them? Most psychologists believe that they are learned early in life and reaffirmed as we get older. In our sexually enlightened age, little children are still likely to be discouraged from touching or playing with their own or each other's genitals. Many parents still feel uncomfortable talking to their children about sex; they either avoid the subject or discuss it so carefully that the child still picks up the feeling that something is not really *right* about sexual pleasure. As adults we may experience this guilt and discomfort with our own sexual pleasure more directly in the postintercourse period:

After having a series of orgasms, I often feel a little nauseous. (woman, 38)

Although I always have an orgasm I feel a bit let down, and not very happy. (man, 36)

I feel a certain malaise. (man, 41)

Why should anyone feel nauseous, let down, or a sense of malaise when there is no obvious reason? When we say we feel nauseous, we are far more likely to be experiencing guilt than digestive problems. When we say we feel vaguely unhappy or experience malaise, we usually do not quite know what is wrong. People may try to find suitable explanations for this inarticulate discontent they feel after sex: The weather is not quite right, the setting is not quite right, the sheets are crumpled or not tucked in enough or tucked in too much. But if this vague discontent usually settles in after intercourse, chances are the explanation is guilt—you are punishing yourself for whatever pleasure you experienced during intercourse or orgasm. Clearly this is a case where you are being your own worst enemy.

There is so much in our culture which contributes to and supports these feelings. Our society stresses that what is most constructive and socially useful requires work; that pleasure is something to be put off, suppressed or not experienced. It is surprising that more of us *don't* feel guilt after intercourse. We suspect, however, that often the manifestations of guilt are not extreme enough to make us feel unhappy—just enough to keep us from experiencing fully the joys of afterplay.

Tired and Drained

Considering how many people leave sex as the very last possible activity of the day, it's not surprising that a high proportion of them feel tired after making love—they are often ready to sleep before they begin. Other people may be in poor physical condition, in which case the vigorous activity, the exercise of sex, is likely to leave them exhausted. People in reasonably good physical shape can feel exhausted after sexual intercourse, no matter what the time of day:

After an orgasm I am usually so exhausted that I barely have the strength for anything else. I usually put my all into having sex, and therefore am pretty exhausted afterwards. My partner is a very hyper person and sometimes I have to make it too clear that I have to be left alone to rest. (man, 25)

I feel drained of energy—somewhat let down. I like to rest. (woman, 27)

Many of the conflicts which make us tired are not fully conscious. We may be suspicious of our partner's sighs, guilty over fantasizing about someone else during the lovemaking, annoyed with our partner's movements, or insecure about our own "performance." These feelings and others like them may be experienced as vague apprehensions we are simply unable to articulate clearly, even to ourselves. We know about these inner conflicts but at the same time we don't want to know about them. This, in itself a conflict, can be exhausting. A war within requires so much energy that there is little left for anything else. And sleep is such a good escape. You may want to pay attention to your partner, but just keeping your eyes open is a struggle. You are simply exhausted, and the next thing you know it is morning:

I am somewhat drained of emotion. (man, 36)

I am very tired but somewhat close to my partner. (man, 20)

I feel completely drained and tired. (man, 29)

I usually feel tired after intercourse. I usually rest for a while or go to sleep. In the afternoon I nap, at night I go to sleep. (woman, 27)

The following is a case of an intelligent, successful, but not very happy man. Walter, like many of us, has difficulty being intimate with his family and friends.

I don't know

Walter H., a 38-year-old physician, has been married for ten years to a 35-year-old business woman. They have no children.

Walter gets up early almost every morning to jog three miles before going to his office. During these solitary times, he usually thinks extensively about his professional plans. His evenings are spent reading and listening to music. He rarely socializes with friends.

For some time now, Walter's marriage has not been a happy one. Although he does not find his sexual relationship to be a satisfying, positive experience, he has not yet discussed the problem with his wife.

After intercourse, Walter and his wife usually separate almost immediately. He generally feels "exhausted" and either reads or falls asleep. He feels that his wife wants to be alone following intercourse, although, in fact, she would probably prefer caressing and conversation to separation. Walter himself is unhappy with the status quo.

Their postcoital period involves no tenderness or sharing. When they do speak, it usually is about some daily event. Walter, who feels he might enjoy some quiet conversation and occasionally more sex, has not indicated these desires to his wife. When asked what most attracted him to his partner, Walter replied, "I don't know."

Walter's afterplay would, obviously, be greatly improved by some communication with his wife—as would his marriage. If that happened, we doubt that he would often feel "exhausted" after sex.

After intercourse everyone occasionally feels tired and goes to sleep. But we wonder why so many people stack the odds in favor of exhaustion and sleep. Why is sex so often the last possible activity of the day? For some it is simply habit. For others, it may be a way of avoiding the intimacy of afterplay. Fortunately, whether the reason for it is habit or avoidance, the behavior can be changed. By making love earlier and engaging in activities other than sleep, afterplay can become memorable.

Relaxed

Shere Hite reported in 1976 that women feel one of two ways after orgasm: "tender and loving, wanting to be close" and "strong and wide awake, energetic and alive." Hite says that these feelings after orgasm are similar to the feelings of arousal that women have in foreplay.[5] But we found that the one word used most often by both women and men to describe their postcoital feelings was "relaxed." In fact, the percentage of women stating that they felt relaxed was even higher than that of men.

I feel relaxed, refreshed, and things are low for me so I just take it easy. (man, 23)

Generally, after a session of intercourse, I feel "mellow" and like to relax. (man, 26)

I just like lying in bed and relaxing. (woman, 28)

I have a feeling of well-being and relaxation. (woman, 32)

The physiological changes which mark the passage from orgasm to afterplay seem to go with the subjective feelings of relaxation so commonly experienced. Masters and Johnson have reported that during orgasm, respiratory rates for both sexes may exceed 40 per minute (normal is about 20 or less), and that cardiac rates run from 100 to beyond 180 beats per minute (the normal range is from 60 to 80). In the postorgasmic period both men and women return to their normal physiological states. This means that generally there is a loss of tension and a return to normal breathing, heart rate, and blood pressure. The genitals also return to their normal size and color.[6] Most people do feel relaxed.

But feelings of relaxation cannot properly be understood without reference to the context. Take a close look at the two groups of similar comments that follow. In the first group we hear from three men, then from five women:

I merely feel satisfied, not ecstatic or transfigured. I usually feel more relaxed, less "preoccupied," because I satisfied my sex urge and can then go on to other things. (man, 30)

I have a feeling of release and relaxation. (man, 39)

I feel relaxed and drained of energy. (man, 39)

Usually I feel relaxed and sleepy after intercourse. (woman, 24)

I just lay back and relax and drift off to sleep. (woman, 26)

Sometimes I feel relaxed and exhausted. (woman, 22)

Having sex is very relaxing and seems to release a lot of tensions in the day. (woman, 24)

Usually I feel released—like my excess energy has been used and I feel calmer. (woman, 22)

In this next group of comments, the first two are from men and the last five from women:

Usually I feel relaxed after sex and more comfortable. (man, 22)

I feel very relaxed and good afterward—the traditional afterglow. (man, 25)

I feel relaxed and content after intercourse. (woman, 32)

Most of the time my feelings are very relaxed and very good. (woman, 44)

I feel relaxed and peaceful. (woman, 31)

If it's daytime, I linger in that space of relaxation as long as I can before doing what I have to do. (woman, 22)

I feel good after intercourse. I usually relax. (woman, 32)

In comparing these two groups of comments in which people described themselves as feeling relaxed after intercourse, we can see that for some this means feeling groggy or sleepy, whereas for others it means something more positive—feeling peaceful and *good.*

More than a third of our sample used the word "relaxed" in their description of postintercourse feelings, and feeling relaxed would certainly seem preferable to feeling tense. Yet in many of the reports, where relaxation is the *primary* postcoital feeling, the experience means release or relief rather than joy.

When relaxation is always felt in the context of feeling drained or exhausted, we wonder if the word itself is even appropriate. Such a feeling may actually reflect the same type of problems and conflict we discussed in the previous two sections—if not simple exhaustion. Even in the more positive descriptions, there is no mention of the shared activity or even shared relaxation found in truly satisfying afterplay. The following quote from a 25-year-old woman is a particularly vivid example of the "turning inward" that for some people characterizes the relaxation of the postcoital period:

I feel loose and completely relaxed within myself. I feel turned into my body, focusing on my body and treating it to something good.

Feeling relaxed is mentioned so often probably because it is in such marked contrast to our usually tense emotional lives. The major neurosis of our time is obsessional thought. Particular neurotic symptoms do seem to occur in particular places and times. For example, hysterical fainting and hysterical paralysis, symptoms with no physiological explanations, were much more prevalent in Victorian Europe than they are today in the United States. In America today we don't normally faint, but we do normally have trouble relaxing— "turning off our minds." How often has this happened to you? You lie awake thinking of what someone said or did, or what you should or shouldn't have said or done. When you want to relax and go to sleep, you cannot get rid of the ideas going around and around in your mind. Obsessional neurosis—the inability to control one's own thoughts—is such a common affliction of our time that it is unusual to find someone who is not plagued at least occasionally by these disturbing symptoms.

The postintercourse period is for many people a short but welcome respite from the problem. They feel less worried, less anxious, less concerned, and less obsessed.

There is no question but that it is wonderful to feel calm and relaxed, and the postcoital period offers us the opportunity to experience these feelings. It provides us, as well, with an even greater opportunity—if we remember that we are with someone else. Relaxation shared with one's partner is relaxation plus. And when other activities and emotions are shared in afterplay, even deeper and more enjoyable experiences are possible.

Energized

Many of our accepted, largely unquestioned, attitudes and beliefs about sexuality have little basis in fact, although they may exercise considerable influence over our sexual feelings and behavior. If you or your partner actually believe, for example, that "penis size determines a man's sexual effectiveness," or that "vaginal orgasms are more 'mature' than clitoral ones," that belief is going to affect your sex life—and not for the better.

The same thing goes for the belief that people are always sleepy after intercourse. If you believe that sleeping is what people do, you'll be less likely to do much else yourself. We have found that not only does everyone not feel sleepy after sex, but some people feel energized:

I feel free and open—generally wide awake and if it is at night I enjoy the dark quietness of sitting up in bed and thinking. (woman, 34)

I feel very energetic and talk a lot or get up and do things. (woman, 34)

Most often I feel refreshed and awake and excited. (woman, 31)

I am usually wide awake after intercourse. (woman, 40)

I usually feel exhilarated after and want to begin planning work for the following day. (man, 24)

Once in a while I am seized by energy, particularly after intercourse—feel like getting up and doing things. (woman, 26)

Sometimes I feel very creative after sex. I occasionally write a song or a poem at that time. (man, 33)

Why do some people feel an increase rather than an ebbing of energy after intercourse? Perhaps it is because a majority in this group are very satisfied with their afterplay. Their excitement may come from feeling especially happy with themselves and their partners at that time.

I feel great exhilaration and she looks at me as if I might be "teched." I joke, scurry about, lie back down, chatter a mile a minute. It's a natural high for me. Often I can get up after 30 minutes and grade four hours of research papers in 45 minutes. Wow! (man, 37)

I feel satisfied, loved, alive, vibrant, happy, gratified, and respected. (man, 63)

I feel loving and gentle but energized. (woman, 30)

Of course these people do not *always* feel "up" after intercourse, nor are we suggesting that this is necessarily a preferred state. What we do learn from these people is that there is no inevitable state of being in afterplay, that our experience in the postcoital period is largely determined by culture, learning, and habit. If we believe that lovemaking should be confined to the latest hours of the night or if we have problems outside or in the relationship, we will be tired. But the idea that sex always leads to a lowering or leveling of energy is simply another sexual myth. And myths do die hard. H. I. Lief reported in 1966 that half the students from five Philadelphia medical schools, after three or four years of training, believed masturbation to be a frequent cause of mental illness. More surprisingly, one-fifth of the faculty also shared this view.[7] As for the myth that intercourse has the inevitable physiological consequence of a loss of energy, it has certainly limited our ability to experience the full range of emotional possibilities in afterplay.

Satisfied

In the following quotes we see that for many people—and for different reasons—the primary postcoital feeling is one of satisfaction or contentment:

I usually feel satisfied even though many times I do not reach orgasm. (woman, 19)

I feel satisfied—loved and loving. (woman, 55)

I feel content, peaceful, happy, and optimistic about things that I was pessimistic about. (woman, 31)

Many people who say they feel satisfied seem to locate this experience in their bodies.

I am physically and mentally satisfied. (woman, 21)

I feel almost euphoric, tingling in my body, happy and satisfied. (woman, 19)

I feel physically aware of my body, comfortable, satiated, and satisfied. (man, 21)

I usually feel tingly and really satisfied. (woman, 29)

Fourteen men and twelve women said they feel satisfied after intercourse, and most who did not directly mention the physical aspect of satisfaction alluded to it. Obviously, for many people feelings of satisfaction and contentment develop when there is a diminishing of tension:

I am usually quite relaxed and have an overall feeling of satisfaction. (man, 18)

I feel very relaxed and needed and comfortable and satisfied. (man, 49)

I generally feel relaxed and comfortable, good about myself and good about him. (woman, 22)

Other times I'll get up and pursue some other activity, always with an increased calmness and satisfaction. That lingers for an hour or two. (man, 26)

The emotional benefits of afterplay become clearer as we see these feelings of *combined* satisfaction and relaxation. As a group, people whose primary postcoital feeling is satisfaction or contentment (especially when combined with relaxation) are happy with their overall relationships.

Feeling satisfied does not, of course, necessarily involve the sharing and bonding that constitutes the most rewarding afterplay. It does for the people we are about to discuss—those who feel loved and loving.

Warm, Loved, Loving

Feelings of affection, kindness, and closeness in afterplay are often described as "warmth." Of our sample, 7 men and 24 women specifically said that they felt "warm" after intercourse. Masters and Johnson found that after orgasm, quite aside from the physical exertion in intercourse, there may be a widespread film of perspiration on women's bodies, and sweating on the soles of the feet and the palms of the hands in men.[8] Perhaps the term "warmth" is used so often because the feeling is physical as well as emotional:

Feel mellow, sleepy, warm, satisfied. (man, 35)

I talk, feel relaxed, satisfied, feel warm. (man, 32)

I feel very warm (both emotionally and physically) and loving. (woman, 21)

I feel warn and contented. (woman, 47)

Warm, loving, open to communication. (woman, 31)

I feel very warm all over. (woman, 39)

Warmed, passionate, loving, playful. (woman, 31)

I usually feel very warm, happy, and comfortable. Sex usually puts me in a very good mood. (woman, 24)

Feelings of warmth and sensuality. (man, 27)

I feel warm, loving, comfortable, happy. (man, 33)

Psychologists really don't know very much about love. One explanation of why people feel loving is related to what is called the cognitive theory of emotion. This theory holds that an emotion may be thought of as the name or label we give to a physiological state, depending on the situation we are in. Love then would be seen as occurring when we are highly aroused, as in intercourse and orgasm, and seeking a label for this intense experience. We look at our partner after an almost indescribable feeling and explain the experience to ourselves by saying, "I must love you." For many people feelings of love may well "grow," in this sense, out of states in which they are highly aroused physiologically. But the theory doesn't seem adequate, to say the least. Many people can be highly sexually aroused or fulfilled without feeling love. And we certainly may love someone who does not arouse us physically.

Abraham Maslow in his book *Motivation and Personality* wrote:

> It is amazing how little the empirical sciences have to offer on the subject of love. Particularly strange is the silence of psychologists, for one might think this to be their particular obligation. . . . It is as if we were at the most advanced position in no man's land, at a point where conventional techniques of orthodox psychological science are of very little use. And yet our duty is clear. We must understand love. . . .⁹

Feeling loved and loving—whatever the reason—is an especially wonderful experience in afterplay, as we can see in the following case:

Beautiful and young and full of love

Melissa D. lives with her children in a suburb of Seattle. She is separated, in her mid-40s, lists her occupation as social worker, and says her principal (and only) sexual partner is a married corporate executive. They have been having an affair for seven years.

She describes herself as very satisfied with every aspect of the relationship, and she believes that her partner feels the same way. Hugging and caressing, they praise each other and speak romantically after orgasms (she never fails to reach a climax and has from five to seven of them in an afternoon of lovemaking): "We always lie in each other's arms and talk about ourselves. We're usually very serious and philosophical and we talk about how lucky we are to have each other."

Melissa's ideal afterplay would consist of "candlelight and music and an opulent feast (served by someone). I would like to share eating and drinking from the same plate and glass, and caress and kiss during dinner. I would like my partner to tell me how much he loves me and how beautiful he thinks I am." On the other hand, "the ultimate insult would be for him to move away from me and get up and get dressed. Speaking in a matter-of-fact tone about mundane things would be equally disconcerting."

Her lover, like all men, is not perfect. On those occasions when he does experience sexual difficulties, she always reassures him that "it is not important at all" and that she "enjoys being with him just as much. I praise him for being the best of all lovers and for pleasing me more than anyone in the world."

Although they "often become depressed because we can't be together permanently," she is very happy with both the sexual and overall relationship. They make love once every two or three weeks for about four hours in the afternoon. After lovemaking she feels "beautiful and young and full of love as well as loved. Famished, weak, and shaky directly afterwards and muscle-bound the next day."

"And," she concludes, "I love it!"

As with Melissa's story, in the quotes to follow we can see that the experience of love is the central emotion during afterplay. Unlike Melissa, most of the responses are from people living together or married. Their experiences therefore do not include the kind of depression that Melissa described.

I also feel very loved and wanted; which is very important to me. (woman, 34)

I feel loved and comfortable. (man, 23)

I feel relaxed and loved more and more. (woman, 20)

I feel loving and affectionate and happy and relaxed. (woman, 40)

I feel good. Most of the time sexual encounters bring us emotionally closer and create a loving feeling. (woman, 25)

I feel warm, female, loved, appreciated, relaxed, loving, fulfilled, and in general very close to my man and really good about our life together. (woman, 41)

I feel loved and comforted after having intercourse. (woman, 17)

I usually feel completely relaxed, at least a bit drowsy and overwhelmed with love for my partner, which makes me want to kiss, hug, and hold my partner close to me. (woman, 27)

I feel very loving and needed. (man, 27)

I feel very loving and secure feelings about our relationship. (woman, 19)

I feel contented and loved. I am very aware of my own body and his. (woman, 23)

I feel fulfilled, happy, tingly, and most important—loved. (woman, 21)

Making love to my partner is delicious. I care for her very much afterwards. (man, 21)

I feel warm, emotionally, and caring and loving toward my partner—as well as loved by him. I feel very vulnerable emotionally. (woman, 27)

Twenty women and seven men said they felt love or felt loved after intercourse. It was surprising to us that more people did not report these feelings. Why don't more people feel love after making love? We think it is because love involves more than the satisfaction of strictly sexual needs. Love can be understood, to some extent, as the feeling we have toward someone who satisfies our most important *human* needs. And the desires to have intercourse and orgasm, of course, are not our only needs. We also need to be accepted, with all our limitations; we need to be touched and reassured; to communicate intimately with someone; to share our thoughts, feelings, activities, and lives. The postintercourse period is ideal for the fulfillment of these needs. If the only need fulfilled during the sexual encounter is an orgasmic one, not only will we not feel love, but we may feel used, disappointed, guilty, tired, or alone.

No matter how many times we have intercourse, no matter how "good" it is, we still need to be loved. Ultimately, if we are not loved in the postcoital period there is emptiness. Even if everyone in the whole world pays attention to you, the whole world is not interested in sharing your feelings, your thoughts—your life—so still there is emptiness. If we never feel loved in the vulnerable postintercourse period, we can become acutely aware of its absence in our overall relationship. Inevitably, the most satisfying afterplay involves sharing. In all of the activities to be described in the next chapter you will see that it is the sharing of feelings, thoughts, and activities that is crucial. Love grows out of sharing; the feeling of "I" becomes a feeling of "we." There is such emotional closeness that there is a radical shift in ego boundaries—what hurts your partner hurts you, your joy is your partner's joy. This feeling of "we" is the major part of the experience of love in the postintercourse period. We transcend our usual solitary ego-consciousness. Our consciousness expands to include another. And such an experience may help us make a bridge to a more spiritual plane of consciousness, as we shall now see.

Altered States

The experience of love is one example of a state radically different from our usual way of being in the world. Several respondents described other feelings in the postintercourse period which would best be described as altered states of consciousness. Some of these states, in fact, bear a remarkable similarity to the altered states reported in William James's *The Varieties of Religious Experience*. James himself had direct experience of such a state of consciousness, and his discussion of that experience is a classic in the field:

> One conclusion was forced upon my mind at that time and my impression of its truth has ever since remained unshaken. It is that our normal waking consciousness, rational consciousness as we call it, is but one special type of consciousness, while all about it, parted from it by the filmiest of screens, there lie potential forms of consciousness entirely different. We may go through life without suspecting their existence; but apply the requisite stimulus and at a touch they are there in all their completeness, definite types of mentality which probably somewhere have their field of application and adaptation. No account of the universe in its totality can be final which leaves these other forms of consciousness quite disregarded.[10]

For James, the parting of the filmy screen to different forms of consciousness was brought about by nitrous oxide, the particular form of consciousness induced being an experience of reconciliation. "It is as if the opposites of the world whose contradictories and conflict make all our difficulties and troubles, were melted into unity."[11]

In the quotes and case below, we see that for some people orgasm and its aftermath bring about recognizably altered states of consciousness. For some, these can best be described as states of oneness and unity.

Sometimes I am truly into the afterglow. To feel as one with my partner. At least the feeling of transcending the individual being so that we both derive joy of being united through the act of making love. (man, 21)

I feel completely relaxed and content. I feel sensations all over my body. It is such a completely different and unique experience, so beautiful that I can just lie there and feel it all over. I don't want it to leave, it's the greatest feeling you can feel. (woman, 30)

I feel as though I am on a different and more pleasant plane. I feel so warm and content. (woman, 26)

I have tingles all over my body. I feel as though we are in a different world—our own world impervious to the usual and outside world. (woman, 18)

The "oneness" described below by Laura R. is truly the ultimate afterplay experience, an experience we think is accessible to all of us.

We whisper

Laura R., 23, has been involved in an ongoing relationship with her 24-year-old boyfriend for several years now. Although they have separate apartments, they almost always spend their nights together, often waking up to morning lovemaking. Their frequent intercourse includes long periods of foreplay which they both enjoy considerably. Laura usually reaches an orgasm.

For Laura it is the time after sex when she feels most fully the strength of her relationship with her lover. "I generally feel *very* happy due to the feeling of unity between my partner and myself. The bonds of physical togetherness fade away, transcended by a tighter bond of emotional and mental 'oneness'. . . . I think I enjoy these moments almost the best of all. I feel so much love come through when we cuddle."

Lying close together, they enjoy ". . . feeding each other while continuing to nibble on one another as well. Shoulder massages are exchanged, as are warm deep kisses. . . . I put perfume behind his ears and then kiss him there. He rubs my foot and nibbles my toes. We whisper, hold hands, and communicate our love for each other."

Laura hates to spoil this time by "spacing out and thinking about problems or worrying about trivial things." For her this should be a time of leisure—having to rush off, even to get up to go to the bathroom, is a totally unwelcome intrusion. She prefers to let the experience speak for itself, hating "after-intercourse discussions about 'performance,' the ugly 'how was I' line."

Other respondents also described feelings of unity or whole-ness, sometimes as the synthesis or joining of opposites:

I lie in bed just floating and enjoying the euphoric state of being and non-being. (man, 25)

I feel calm, safe, and very whole. (woman, 23)

I feel completed. It is an emotional climax with feelings of despondence, joy, emptiness, and fullness all at the same time. (woman, 28)

I stop thinking and fantasizing; stop any mental activities. I seem to enjoy my senses more and use them as fully as possible. I feel very satisfied and whole. (man, 26)

For some the postintercourse period is a time of disrupting routines, disrupting their usual way of feeling and seeing the world.

I feel like I am really seeing things. It's as though we have stopped the world for a while. (woman, 24)

What seems to be occurring for these people is what might best be described as a mystical experience. This type of experience cannot be explained logically or demonstrated openly—any more than the feeling of nostalgia can be explained to a young child, or the perception of green to a person who is color blind, or the experience of love to someone who has never known it. These experiences may be difficult to talk about and more difficult to study, but it does not make them any less real or important. The altered states of consciousness reported by people in the postintercourse period share much with William James's account of the mystical experience which he sees as the center of the religious experience. James says that such a state is characterized by four basic qualities. First, it is ineffable. This means that it defies expression. To be understood it must be experienced directly. Second, the experience is perceived as being full of significance and importance. Third, although activity may bring on such a state, volition or will plays a relatively unimportant role. Last, these states are not sustained for long; they are typically transient.[12]

These "basic qualities" show up in some of our respondents' descriptions of their state of mind after lovemaking. All four qualities can be recognized in the quotes that follow:

I feel like a trillion bucks, very whole, very elated, very in love, very high into life. Before sex was either an obligation or just a novelty but never a religious experience as I have recently found it to be. (man, 20)

Although these feelings don't last long, I feel a calmness and a wholeness which is quite indescribable. When my wife and I share these feelings I can only say that it is like seeing God. (man, 36)

Simultaneously I feel my love, my partner's love and the love all around us. It is delicious ecstasy. (woman, 40)

We realize, of course, that not everyone is interested in reaching mystical states of consciousness. But our respondents have made it clear that unusual and exciting positive experiences are possible in the postcoital period. When we began our research we were aware that most people do not take full advantage of this time; we did not realize how rich and varied this experience can be for many men and women.

Changing Your Feelings

Perhaps you are one of the many people whose typical feelings in the postintercourse period are among the negative ones we've described. Or perhaps you feel all right after sex, but you now realize that you could feel even better. What can you do?

We human beings are complicated. Our thoughts, feelings, and actions are inextricably intertwined. Change in one almost invariably leads to change in the others. This means that if we change our thoughts and behavior, our feelings will also change. In fact, many psychologists now believe that the fastest and most effective way to change feelings is to change thoughts, actions, or both. For example, if you cannot study or work and feel anxious, it is probably true that by eliminating anxiety you would be able to work more effectively. But "eliminating anxiety" is no easy task. The alternative, learning ways to study or work more effectively, is likely to be far easier. And increased effectiveness could lead you to think more positively about yourself and thus feel less anxious.

The same rationale applies to improving your experience in afterplay. You might say your afterplay is not good *because* you aren't relaxed or your partner isn't relaxed. Or you might take the view that "if our relationship was good our afterplay would be good too." You could be right, but if so you are stuck. You cannot order yourself or your partner to feel relaxed (think how you would feel if someone said, "YOU MUST RELAX!"), and trying to change a whole relationship is a near-impossible task. What is a relationship anyway? Isn't it made up of all those moments you spend with your partner, some of the most important of which are spent in bed, during afterplay? Perhaps if you change what you *do* in those moments, you will change your feelings. And if you feel good during afterplay there is a very good chance that you will feel good the next morning.

The way to feel good is not to keep saying to yourself "I will feel good, I will feel good." It is to do the kinds of things that make you feel good, and to avoid doing the things that make you feel bad. We do not know exactly what these are for you, but we know what they are for the hundreds of people we surveyed. What they had to say is presented in the next two chapters. Perhaps you will find some appealing ideas in Chapter 5 and some mistakes to avoid in Chapter 6. For now, don't worry about your feelings. Think about what you and your partner do, see if you can begin to change that, and the feelings might just take care of themselves.

CHAPTER 5

What People Like

Some readers might appreciate a clear formula as to what should or shouldn't be done after sex. Pronouncements like "All men like having their backs scratched" or "All women like to be told they are beautiful" would offer a sense of security about what to do—a false sense, however, since people are unique.

One of the greatest American psychologists, the late Gordon Allport, pointed out that psychologists face special problems as they attempt to explore human behavior and experience. Scientists have always looked for common properties in the things they investigate. Chemists examine the properties, not of this or that piece of iron, but of iron in general. Botanists attempt to make general statements about leaves. But what is most striking about *people* is not their similarities but their differences. Each of us is indeed unique.[1] If you live with someone for a long while or get to know him or her well, how would you respond if someone asked, "Who does he (she) remind you of?" You could not answer. When you know a person well enough, he or she is unique and does not remind you of anyone else.

And yet there are similarities. There are certain things that many of us like or do not like. Some of this is codified as law (for example, few of us like to be robbed, and there are laws against robbery). Much is part of our social rules. We know, for example, that most people like to be thanked for gifts, and we act accordingly. And, thanks to the many books on sexuality, we know what constitutes—for many of us—ideal foreplay. Different as we are from one another, there are certain stimulating touches *practically* everyone enjoys.

We found a similar situation in the case of afterplay. When we asked people to describe their ideal afterplay, we got 250 different answers. In those answers, however, certain behaviors and environments were mentioned by many respondents. What is ideal for them may turn out to be highly pleasurable for you.

In presenting what men and women say they most like to do after sex, we have to point out that for some people this ideal situation is clearly a fantasy. On occasion we found a large discrepancy between what people actually do and what they want to do, between what their partners say and do and they want them to say and do, between the atmosphere that exists and the atmosphere that is desired. In these situations, you find unhappy afterplayers. Fortunately, for other people there is a closer correspondence between what they do and feel after sex, and their ideal situation.

The gap between afterplay as it is and afterplay as it is desired is one excellent measure of how satisfied we are with our postintercourse behavior and experience. For most people, closing this gap is not difficult. In the pages that follow, we hope you will find some new possibilities for yourself. Good afterplay is easy and is its own reward. Just being aware of the fact that there is a postintercourse period—and that it is a special time with your partner—should make you a better afterplayer. The information that follows, which comes out of the feelings and thoughts of our diverse sample, will also help.

When people described their ideal afterplay (in Question 41

and in interviews), nine factors emerged. At least a few respondents mentioned each factor and some of the nine were mentioned by nearly everybody.

These elements of ideal afterplay are:

Touch
Loving words
Conversation
Relaxation
Privacy and quiet
Soft lights and music
Different surroundings
Bathing
Food and drink

Touch

More than any other factor, people mentioned close physical contact as part of their ideal afterplay. How often do we find ourselves at so intimate a distance as when we make love? In the course of a day such physical proximity is rare, unless we frequent crowded elevators and subway trains—in which case we often feel our personal space to be violated. As Edward Hall points out in his book *The Hidden Dimension*, when people are less than six inches from each other they are likely to be making love, wrestling, comforting, or protecting.[2] All these activities can be a part of afterplay.

This rare closing of physical distance following sex permits us to use our senses in a way which we use infrequently or not at all. We can smell each other, taste each other, and feel each other. The appropriate forms of communication at this intimate distance usually do not include the most often used channels. Vision is neither sharp nor sharply focused, and words are often unnecessary and too loud. Particularly in the moments just following intercourse, looking and talking are less effective means of communication. But we can experience each other sensually and perhaps more fundamentally.

A great deal can be communicated through touch. Some animals, like chimpanzees, touch each other's genitals to give reassurance and comfort. Certainly in the postintercourse period we can touch to reassure (although genital touches may be painful or uncomfortable at this time). We can also reinforce, stimulate, protect, comfort, admire, and love through touch. The laying on of hands has always been a part of medical practice. Touch heals.

We can listen to and feel each other's breath and heartbeat. We can feel and touch not only with our hands but with our feet, cheeks, noses, thighs, and lips.

For some of the many people who mentioned intimate physical contact in their descriptions of what they wanted after intercourse, the desired contact was of an active sort—massage, scratching, etc.:

Shoulder massages are exchanged, as are deep, warm kisses. We continue to touch and be beside one another. (woman, 21)

I like cuddling and being complimented on my body as it is stroked. I like stroking my partner where he enjoys it (forehead, neck and upper chest). I like to have my back scratched and massaged and my hair brushed or rubbed. (woman, 30)

Not to talk but hold each other a short while and have my head or back rubbed. (woman, 26)

After we had lain together momentarily enjoying "the warm glow" he would stroke me—my back, neck, massage me gently all over— hold me tight and then release again and again. Just general touching, loving, warm movements and gestures. (woman, 26)

I like him to just lie next to me, hugging and caressing me for awhile. I also like him to massage me and vice versa. (woman, 17)

To speak not at all. To hug very tightly, then to lie quietly and have my mate touch me, rub my head and scratch my back. (man, 33)

My ideal after-intercourse experience involves the affection and tender attention of my partner. I enjoy hugging and kissing in general after intercourse (a massage—preferably full body—would be heaven). (woman, 25)

The ideal after-intercourse experience for me involves a continuation of massaging and continued contact. (man, 63)

I like to be close to my partner; I like physical contact. I like him to kiss me and hold me, rub my back and play with my hair. (woman, 30)

I would like to be held and caressed for an hour and then given a body rub with oil and hot towels. (woman, 31)

I like to be so close that I can feel and hear her breathing. I like to touch her hair and feel her long nails go up and down my back and legs. (man, 36)

Touching need not, of course, necessarily be in the form of massage. Hugging, kissing and caressing were mentioned very often by our respondents:

I like him to stay inside me for awhile, then remain close with gentle caresses. (woman, 21)

I like intimate caressing. Nothing would have to be said. (man, 35)

I enjoy being gently touched and caressed by her. (man, 21)

I would like my partner to continue to hold me close and caress me. (woman, 32)

I love caressing, kissing and holding. (woman, 23)

I like to have him stay inside me, and to hug and kiss me. (woman, 34)

Most of all I enjoy being held and kissed. (woman, 24)

I would consider being close, naked, touching and hugging the ideal after-intercourse experience. (woman, 24)

I like to lie around and hold one another and just feel that gentle glow of trust and love that comes after satisfying sex with someone I am close to. (woman, 22)

As we have said, the postcoital period seems to be a time of heightened vulnerability. People need the reassurance communicated through touch; they want to know through physical and sensual experience that there is intimacy in the relationship that goes beyond the orgasm. This need for reassurance is clear in the following comments:

Right after we've had sex, I want my partner to be as loving and as affectionate as before. (woman, 29)

I would like to feel he had a continued desire to touch and be with me. I need caresses as assurances that the sex was good and that there is depth to our intimacy—and that the intimacy can continue. (woman, 33)

Just after intercourse, I like to be held and caressed either verbally or physically and to feel that it is important to my husband that it is me who is there. (woman, 32)

The ideal experience for me would be one of a quiet and emotional nature. My partner need not say anything, but rather show his love for me by tenderly holding and caressing me, by making me feel as if I am the only person alive (at least in that moment). (woman, 27)

Two terms very often used in descriptions of ideal post-intercourse behavior were "snuggle" and "cuddle." These words seem to capture the flavor of warm, loving postintercourse contact.

I like warm cuddles with kisses. I want to be held and to share dreams with one another. (woman, 25)

I love to snuggle. (woman, 26)

I like to be held and cuddled. (woman, 34)

I like to lie there together with our arms wrapped around one another, snuggling and cuddling, with his head on my shoulder or breasts. (woman, 25)

I like the kissing, hugging, holding, and snuggling the best. (woman, 28)

When postcoital contact and touching is prolonged, there is always the possibility that afterplay can become foreplay. When this occurs, afterplay can occur more than once in the same lovemaking session. For some people, this turn of events is ideal:

And then I would enjoy more lovemaking. (woman, 41)

I like oral sex after intercourse. (woman, 20)

I like to be held and caressed and start foreplay again. (woman, 32)

This will sound a little selfish, but some very gentle postintercourse head and general licking is always very nice. (man, 25)

I like doing things that lead to more sex without feeling pressured to respond. (man, 35)

I like my partner to put back on her sexy negligee and begin to turn me on again and I begin to turn her on again. (man, 31)

I like to hold and caress my lover and have him do the same. I like for him to kiss my breasts and neck. I love to lick and kiss his thighs and lower abdomen and feel him get hard again in my hands. Making love again is wonderful. (woman, 39)

Various kinds of close physical contact were listed as desirable afterplay for both the men and women in our sample. Fifty people specifically mentioned cuddling, kissing and hugging; forty-four people spoke of caressing and fondling. Twenty-two stressed the importance of being close and warm, while nineteen people mentioned massages or backrubs. If you do not already touch in these ways after sex, we suggest that you try them. Certainly you will be likely to please your partner—who may well reciprocate your physical attentiveness.

In the following case we can see how massage and other kinds of loving attentiveness can play a central part in the afterplay experience. It is interesting to note that Louise's one problem is that she is doing exceptionally well sexually, without quite realizing it. She has orgasms regularly, but feels that she should be having vaginal ones, and although she enjoys long periods of postcoital contact, she views her afterplay experience as typical rather than special.

I don't think we do anything unusual

When 28-year-old Louise T. describes negative postcoital experiences, she is not talking about her 27-year-old husband. What she would dislike is "a partner jumping out of bed after he has come, critical comments on my performance or on my body, being ignored either verbally or physically, or having to rush to get dressed to go out." But what she likes—and gets—from her husband is positive attention, both physical and verbal:

"We lie in each other's arms—usually me in the crook of his arm. We stroke one another—I feel relaxed, mellow, very close to him. I like to see his relaxed face and listen to his breathing on the side of his chest. Sometimes we compliment each other on a specific technique used during lovemaking."

She continues, "I like soft classical music and candlelight, or watching the sunset . . . cuddling and being complimented on my body as it is stroked . . . stroking my partner where he enjoys it (i.e., forehead, neck, and upper chest) . . . to hear words about his caring and love for me . . . to have my back scratched or massaged and my hair brushed or rubbed."

Louise's only concern about her sexual life is that her orgasms (which occur nearly every time she and her husband have sex) are "only clitoral, not vaginal ones." Her expectations of vaginal orgasms have led her to be somewhat disappointed with intercourse itself, but she remains happy with the sexual relationship.

Both Louise and her husband are busy people—she as a librarian, he as a psychologist. But still, after eight years of marriage, they lie together hugging and caressing for up to an hour after intercourse. For Louise this is perfectly natural. As she says in her concluding comment, "I don't think we do anything unusual after intercourse."

Loving Words

During sex our feelings, emotions, and actions are experienced and expressed with immediacy and a high degree of emotional intensity. Orgasm involves a "letting go" which is more than a physical release. Roles, masks, status all fall away, exposing a part of us much more basic and natural—and vulnerable. It should therefore not be surprising that many people need not only to feel accepted through touch and caress, but to hear verbal acceptance, praise, reassurance, and validation. A cruel or uncaring word or phrase can be devastating at this time, even as the expression of love and tenderness can be psychologically strengthening.

In the postintercourse period, we have the rare opportunity to affirm and accept each other's sexuality and sensuality. We can also reinforce each other's sexual behavior and experience. For certainly the consequences of a behavior have been shown to determine the probability of that behavior's occurring in the future. Intercourse or orgasm may be followed by praise, affection and warmth or by lack of interest; in either case the effect on future sexual relations, behaviors, and feelings will be profound. And if that effect is negative enough, over a long enough period of time, we will be likely to have less sex—or more likely to seek reinforcement for our sexuality elsewhere. In the quotes that follow, the need for reinforcement is stated, in many different ways, over and over again:

I would like my partner to tell me how much he loves me and how beautiful he thinks I am. (woman, 41)

I like to be told nice things. (woman, 32)

I like romantic talk and maybe some compliments. (woman, 32)

I would like to talk about how beautiful it was making love. I would like to hear something wonderful my partner thought or felt about me. (woman, 40)

The questionnaire brings the realization that both my partner and myself spend little time after lovemaking in complimenting each other. And I really enjoy compliments and "love talk." This is something for me to consider. (woman, 25)

I like reinforcement. (woman, 22)

If we had a particularly nice time, I'd like him to comment on it. I would like to hear him speak romantically . . . but not if that was the only time, as I would feel suspicious. My current partner and I do not have that as an element of our relationship, but I guess that would be part of an ideal after-intercourse experience for me. (woman, 23)

I like saying loving things to each other. I like my partner to tell me he enjoyed it (especially if it was oral sex) and that he thought I was sexy or "good." (woman, 19)

I would love to have my husband tell me over and over again how much he loves me. (woman, 26)

I love you. (woman, 32)

I enjoy letting my partner know how much I love her and having her do the same. (man, 26)

The ideal would be for my partner to always, but truthfully, express his satisfaction. The more pleasure I give him, the more I feel pleased. (woman, 26)

I would want to be held close and told that I was cared for, as well as how wonderful I was in bed. (woman, 19)

Listening to my mate tell me how much he loves me, how he can't live without me and other sweet and loving nice things in my ear. (woman, 24)

I like to feel she thought I was the greatest. (man, 60)

I find it ideal to be told I am beautiful, a great lover, and I am loved. (woman, 19)

Most of all for him to say he loves me. (woman, 21)

I like to hear words of love and endearment and also that I am the only one—fidelity. (woman, 27)

I like telling each other how we feel about each other. I would like him to tell me how beautiful I am and how great in bed he thinks I am. (woman, 25)

The only thing my partner should say is I love you, need you and enjoy making love to you. (woman, 27)

My partner should speak endearingly, praise me, make me feel that I am most important in fulfilling his needs. (woman, 32)

There is very little I want after intercourse. I do want a little feedback on our sex together or some complimentary comments on me—how my spouse sees me as a person, a loved person. (woman, 31)

Just say 'I love you!' (woman, 40)

I like feedback that it was satisfying for him as well as his concern of how it was for me. I like to be told I am loved. (woman, 22)

I like to talk, embrace and say how good the lovemaking was and that she was very satisfied. (man, 26)

I like him to tell me he enjoys me; I like to hear sweet things. (woman, 30)

Knowing that my partner has been satisfied and is happy gives me a tremendous amount of pleasure. (man, 27)

I like to be told positive things (I love you, I love to make love to you, you're a great lay). (woman, 27)

I like to hear loving words including my name or pet names. (woman, 38)

I feel really good about my partner and feel "Why don't you tell me you love me?" That's the one thing—with all those good feelings, I just wish he'd verbalize it more. (woman, 28)

It's really great to hear your name said—it makes a difference. But the name has to be your name. (woman, 24)

Forty-one respondents said they especially like to speak or hear romantic words. And many said they enjoy being complimented and praised as part of afterplay—although it seems not to happen as much as it is desired. For example, only 12 people stated in essay question 40 (What do you do . . .) that after sex they say they love their partners, whereas 27 people said that to hear such words would be a part of ideal afterplay.

Unfortunately many of our most positive feelings toward each other go unexpressed. We may feel wonderful just being with someone, but we don't tell them how we feel. There seem to be plenty of reasons for this holding back. Perhaps if you tell your lover how good he or she feels to hold, or how good you feel, you might sound corny or inflate his/her ego. Or if the sex was not that good for your partner and you say it was marvelous, you will be making a fool out of yourself. Or if you feel wonderful, your partner must know—so why say anything?

Fears like these are, of course, poor reasons for holding back on communicating your feelings. "Not wanting to sound corny" is often an excuse for being afraid to express positive emotions, a fear you're better off overcoming than giving in to. A surprisingly few people suffer from the problem of ego inflation— the reverse is much more common—which makes it difficult to compliment too much. If the sex was not that good for your partner and you say it was wonderful for you, he or she will be likely to get some gratification in knowing that you feel good. And, finally, remember that most people cannot read minds. If you feel good your partner may not know just how you feel, and even if he or she does know, hearing it can be lovely.

People do not like to be compared with other lovers. Sex is not a performance to be appraised, nor do we like to feel that we are being rated or evaluated. But most of us *do* like to hear compliments—if they're honest. Half-hearted compliments or praise that isn't justified are worse than nothing at all. Although we like acceptance and reinforcement we do not like being lied to nor do we like feeling manipulated.

As for timing, the expression of honest compliments is most effective and meaningful when given just after intercourse, or just after a period of silent physical contact following sex. When we are as open and as vulnerable as we are in the postintercourse period, the effects of praise and reinforcement are heightened. If you feel wonderful, say so. If your partner looks or feels delicious, let go and tell them and, most of all, if you feel loving, let your partner know.

Conversation

The often-heard statement that communication is important for a good relationship says so much that it doesn't say anything at all. The word "communication" covers judgments, evaluations, accusations, exclamations, explanations, bodily movements, and more. The quotes that are to follow suggest that there is a particular kind of communication that makes for good afterplay—intimate conversation.

In 1936, social psychologist Kurt Lewin studied the extent to which people differ in revealing personal or intimate aspects of themselves. Lewin suggested that we might be pictured as a series of concentric circles, with our more intimate and private thoughts and feelings at the center and our more public ones on the outside.[3] Depending on who we are with, and the situation we find ourselves in, the boundary which separates what we share with others and what we keep to ourselves changes. During afterplay, this boundary can shift so much that much of what is usually private may be available and can be shared. Being stripped of roles, facades, and clothes facilitates intimate, personal, conversation. There is little to hide and little to hide behind. When two people have shared a sexual experience and lie close together, that is not the best time to discuss balancing the check book, getting the car fixed, or the rate of inflation. Intimate communication in afterplay means that through the sharing of sexuality, we trust each other sufficiently to self-disclose—to reveal our feelings, thoughts, hopes, dreams, fears, and memories.

Psychological problems arise whenever we lie to or hide from others who are significant in our lives. This may be one reason why adolescents experience so much psychological turmoil. In the first 12 years of life, the significant "others" for a child are parents, and children typically have little to hide. Later, beginning with the physical and emotional changes of puberty, most children come to feel that they must hide their innermost selves from intrusion by their parents. For many of us this very difficult and painful adjustment does not end with adolescence. If we develop a pattern of living in which we feel so uncomfortable with our thoughts and feelings that we cannot reveal ourselves to others, we feel isolated. We are not in real contact with others and we may even lose contact with ourselves. Not trusting our own thoughts and feelings, we cannot feel good about ourselves.

This condition of isolation is one that brings people to counselors, psychotherapists, and psychiatrists. The whole process of psychotherapy, of becoming psychologically healthy, may be seen in part as the process of revealing oneself fully to a significant other. As Sidney Jourard has pointed out in his book, *Healthy Personality: An Approach from the Viewpoint of Humanistic Psychology*,[4] a healthy person will make himself fully known to at least one other significant human being. Through psychotherapy, a client reveals himself to the therapist, and thereby gets to know himself better and becomes capable of establishing real and more satisfying relationships—capable, that is, of revealing himself to others.

In a research study by Jourard and Lasakow, published in 1958, it was found that women are more likely to disclose themselves than men.[5] Thanks to social and cultural conditioning, women have been shown to be more capable of one-to-one intimate relationships than men, who seem to be more concerned with playing social roles and succeeding in business than they are with intimacy. Since intimate communication and conversation is such an important element in good afterplay, this sex difference is consistent with our finding that women are, for the most part, better afterplayers than men.

Not revealing oneself, wearing a mask, or keeping up a facade, being on constant guard against intrusions into the private sphere, consumes a great deal of energy. Because of this, men are under more stress than women, which may be why they die sooner. As Jourard points out in his article, *Healthy Personality and Self-Disclosure,* "Maybe 'being manly,' whatever that means, is slow suicide."[6]

However easy or difficult self-disclosure and intimacy may be for us, respondents to our questionnaire expressed, again and again, the need for them after lovemaking:

The ideal experience can be anything we share together, whether it's a walk or a movie, etc. Lots of times it's a good time for me to become open and discuss our relationship. I think it's a nice time to share your feelings. (woman, 27)

I would like to share with him some thoughts and feelings I am having. I might want to share something that happened in the day if it seemed special to me. I would like him to do the same. (woman, 40)

I like to laugh and play and express fantasies and dreams. I like to decide together, verbally, when we are ready to either fall asleep or get up to dress or whatever. (woman, 23)

I like communication after sex—real communication. I might be too involved with verbal expression, but that's ok. I don't like talking about me as much as I like talking about the other person. What he thinks, what he's feeling—not necessarily about sex, but about things which are important. (woman, 22)

Talking while we are naked is the ideal hour-after-intercourse experience. Talking not necessarily about sex, but just sharing feelings and thoughts. (woman, 24)

My relationship with my partner is still in the developing stages. The postintercourse period is a very significant time for increasing emotional closeness through conversation. (woman, 32)

I like it to be a time when one can be intimate in a conversational or intellectual way—a time to talk about the things I or my partner think about but don't normally convey to other people—one's life, goals, problems, desires, etc. (man, 33)

I have no real love relationship at this time. When I did, however, the best after-intercourse activity was the caring, sensitive communication that occurred. This special close communication and sharing experience which is really different from the actual sex, makes the sex better. (man, 30)

I like talking about the things we like to do, things or people that are important to us. (woman, 23)

A time for discussing private thoughts and ideas—real sharing. It is a dreamy and relaxed time which is conducive to free talk—things can be discussed that cannot be approached at other times. In this somewhat hypnotic state we can reveal ourselves. (woman, 34)

Lately we have been talking about our baby-to-be. We joke about what he or she must have thought was going on while we were having sex. (man, 37)

I like to share our dreams with one another. (woman, 25)

I mostly just like to have a quiet intimate conversation. (woman, 23)

If I am not with my husband, but a lover, I like to get to know my new partner better. It is easier after sex to talk freely. (woman, 34)

It's nice to talk about things, you feel really close to your partner and it comes easily. (woman, 18)

This is a time of being close, a time to discuss any aspects of your relationship or individual issues that either wants to talk about. (woman, 26)

I enjoy hearing my partner say whatever trivial ridiculous things come to mind—it's a time of lack of inhibition, a comfortable time to do whatever you feel like, or say whatever you feel like. I don't really like activity after sex, I enjoy talking more. (woman, 25)

This is the time for a very relaxed talk with the partner. It is for me important that we don't have to rush to get someplace else. I'd like my partner to understand this longing for this relaxed talk no matter what the subject may be. (woman, 21)

Fifty-five people named "talk" a part of their ideal afterplay. Some indicated that talking specifically about dreams and fantasies was best, while others simply wanted pleasant conversation.

People who are having difficulty in a relationship often say they are "not communicating" with their partners. This cannot be. We are *always* communicating with each other although we may not like the form or content of the communication. As we've said, in the moments following intercourse the most powerful communications can be nonverbal. If someone turns away after sex, this is not a lack of communication, it is a clear and unmistakable message. And, of course, a sigh or a hug is an equally direct message.

But people can communicate with great depth and subtlety through the verbal exchange of thoughts and feelings. Words help to define us as human beings, and the particular words we use are a major part of what makes us who we are. The postintercourse period seems to offer us a special opportunity to partake in this most human of interactions.

The following case shows us how important open and intimate conversation can be in the development of a trusting relationship. Donna had been involved in a number of previous relationships in which postcoital conversation was unsatisfactory. In her present relationship, we see how even if there are sexual difficulties, conversation is used to soothe, reassure, and get to know her partner.

My emotions are more available

Donna M., a 31-year-old cinematographer, has recently begun going out with a 24-year-old medical student. This relationship is still "in the developing stages." Their first sexual encounters were marked by some difficulties. "He had little previous experience. He sometimes had trouble maintaining an erection and he sometimes ejaculated before I reached orgasm." Donna did not discourage her lover on these occasions. In fact, on one occasion she said: "'We'll get past this. This isn't bad for starting out.' This was followed by affectionate hugging and kissing. Another time I said, 'We'll be really great when we get through practicing.' We are."

Donna's postcoital reassurance has certainly helped the relationship. Currently they have sex about once a week. She always has an orgasm and usually has two in a typical lovemaking session. She is very happy with their foreplay, intercourse, and postintercourse experience. It is the last of these that Donna feels is especially important for growth in their relationship.

"I have a feeling of great well-being, relaxation, and emotional closeness," she says. "I am able to talk more easily in areas which are usually closed. We talk about our sexual fantasies, our previous experiences, and our feelings for each other. My emotions are more available and less inhibited in conversation. We explore our personalities, our childhood experiences, music, books, art. We talk about and analyze our interactions with other people. Conversation is most important, but so is continued holding and mild caressing. I also enjoy listening to music and drinking ice water or sometimes wine. Subdued light while lying in bed is best, and privacy is essential."

Donna's enjoyment of the postcoital experience can continue for a long period of time. She and her partner usually hug and caress for 30 minutes to an hour. Her postintercourse experiences with previous partners were not always so positive. Donna did not like a lover to criticize her performance, go to sleep immediately, smoke, argue about something, or leave. Yet, "all of these things have happened with one partner or another." In her present relationship, she feels that the time following intercourse is the most significant time for the development of the emotional relationship with her partner.

In a new relationship, the period following intercourse is often the best time for us to get to know one another. There needn't be anxiety or concern about when, if, or how there is to be sex. When two people who have not yet ever made love are in a situation where sex seems likely, conversation often becomes forced as they begin to concentrate on the physical rather than the mental aspects of each other. A common humorous theme in films and television is the awkward conversation that goes on in the minutes preceding "the move." An almost sure sign that the person you are with is thinking strongly about sex is that he or she does not make a great deal of sense and does not seem to hear what you are saying.

Woody Allen has captured beautifully this presexual discomfort in his film, Annie Hall. He and Annie are on their first date; as they walk toward the restaurant where they will have dinner, he suddenly kisses her. He explains to the somewhat shocked young woman that now they can both relax and enjoy dinner, rather than thinking continually about whether or not they will be making love later.

In the postintercourse period, people can talk about what first attracted them to each other, how they feel, who they are. As a relationship develops over time, there is never a lack of significant feelings and thoughts to be revealed and discussed. But we should point out that intimacy develops gradually.

To speak honestly and intimately does not have to mean

saying things that you know your partner does not want or is not ready to hear. You don't have to force a conversation into areas where you know your partner is closed. This is not intimacy, but may be an assault—even a verbal form of rape. If you want to communicate intimately, gently probe with your words and observe your partner's reactions. Enter only where there is an opening.

Don't forget to listen, either: Communication, like sex, takes two people. If you can really be open to and accepting of what your partner is saying, close communication is more likely to develop.

Finally, remember that you don't have to stop touching. Fortunately, we can touch and talk at the same time.

Relaxing

Involvement with the present moment is an unusual experience for many people. It seems strange to say this, but most of us are not really where we are at any given moment. You may be walking down the street, but your mind may be on what someone said to you yesterday, or what you saw on TV last night, or what you plan to do next week or next year or ten years from now. Many people are not even aware of tasting their food while they eat. You may be eating, but your mind is at the office or at school or in some unspecified place with feelings that are appropriate to the past or the future. Of course, there are times when planning or thinking about the future or past is appropriate and healthy. But there are times when you ought to be where you are.

When we are involved with our senses rather than our thoughts, we are more likely to be where we actually are at the moment. We tend to talk or think about the past or future, but we touch in the present. When we are anxious we are almost invariably in the future—anticipating or projecting. One way, then, to reduce anxiety and tension is to focus on the present moment. The easiest way to do this, the easiest way to relax, is to focus on the senses. A psychologist may treat a patient suffering from anxiety attacks by suggesting that he lie down and *feel* the floor beneath him, or concentrate and pay attention to his breathing, or concentrate on tensing and relaxing different muscle groups. By focusing on our senses we remain in the present, we feel less anxious—we relax.

Nothing involves us with sensation more sharply than sex and afterplay. Nor do snuggles and cuddles require much in the way of planning, anticipating, or thought. Perhaps this is why many people say they feel calmest and most sane after sex. The postintercourse period is no time for thinking about problems and concerns. It is, rather, a time to relax with someone who is probably eager to relax with you.

I like to feel warm and secure and relaxed afterwards and anything that would contribute to this state would be welcome. (woman, 26)

I like everything glowing, then drifting into sleep together. (woman, 19)

I like to cuddle and fall asleep together. (man, 28)

I like a quiet and relaxed atmosphere. (man, 39)

I enjoy being relaxed enough to fall asleep while we embrace. (woman, 22)

I like him to lie next to me. I just like being by his side and feeling comforted and relaxed. (woman, 17)

I would like to prolong the relaxed mellow affectionate mood for awhile. Appropriate relaxing activities would be listening to music, drinking something cool, or lounging in the jacuzzi. I doubt if either of us would feel like doing anything more strenuous than that. (woman, 29)

Relaxed quiet atmosphere would be best with no demands. (man, 22)

I want there to be no rush for either of us to leave. He's very easy to restimulate and I love doing it. (woman, 40)

Thirty-four respondents specifically pointed out that their ideal afterplay involved relaxing or feeling relaxed. A number of people mentioned lying next to each other, and 19 spoke of falling asleep in each other's arms.

There are occasions, of course, when any of us may be tense, overtired, "wound up"—and sex can be an excellent way to unwind. The best afterplay might then be to relax and even to sleep. On the other hand, if you are always so tired after sex that you fall asleep immediately, it may be time to consider why you feel this way. The shared pleasures of the postintercourse period are simply not available to us when we're asleep.

Privacy and Quiet

The atmosphere for afterplay was one of the variables most often mentioned when we asked people to describe their ideal postintercourse experience. Not surprisingly, many respondents stressed the importance of privacy and quiet: Good afterplay means staying with your partner, both physically and psychologically, and it's hard to remain in the intimate space of afterplay when there is the possibility of interruption. After sex, people do not want to worry or be concerned about interruptions, distractions, and loud noises:

I just like to be together, with no interruptions from children or phones, etc. (woman, 32)

I don't like intrusions, I couldn't stand the thought of getting up and doing anything. (man, 26)

The best atmosphere would be where there could be no phone to ring or any other interruptions including sleep. (woman, 30)

I like quiet places. If it's at night, I like soft lighting. I want there to be no rush for either of us to leave. (woman, 40)

A private place is important. I don't like to think we might be disturbed. This is especially true when I am with my lover. After making love, I wouldn't want to even think about her husband coming home. That's why motels and hotels are best. (man, 31)

I especially like it to be warm and quiet, with no children around. (woman, 31)

I prefer the privacy of my or his bedroom rather than a place I am not used to being in, like another person's house. I don't like to feel I might be interrupted. (woman, 23)

I like a safe and private place, whether I am with my husband or my lover. (woman, 29)

Thirty-three people indicated their desire for a private or even a secluded atmosphere for afterplay, and twenty-six said it was important that there be no distractions. The adjectives most often used to describe the ideal environment were: quiet, peaceful, warm, cozy, luxurious, romantic, and sexy. A fair number of people specifically said that they disliked being interrupted by the phone, the doorbell, or by children. As will be discussed in the next chapter, a little planning can usually assure you a sufficient amount of time unspoiled by these familiar interruptions.

With a little more planning, you can follow Masters and Johnson's suggestion (in *The Pleasure Bond*) that couples try to take occasional vacations without the children.[7] This can even be done for one night. One man in his mid-30s told us that his in-laws took care of their grandchild while he and his wife spent a very romantic and sexy evening, night, and morning at a nearby motel.

"We really love our son very much," he said, "and in fact we often talk about him after we make love. But it was nice having the privacy for a change. Everyone had a good time."

Soft Lights and Music

From the very beginning of our lives, we are all affected by sound and light. In 1934, L. A. Weiss did an experiment with infants demonstrating that a quiet, continuous noise level produces a quieter, more pacified infant than does silence.[8] It has also been established that babies cry more and sleep less in a totally quiet environment than they do when a radio is playing. Newborns are also affected by light, staying quieter when there is a little of it than when they are in total darkness.

Other research has examined the ways in which music and lighting affect work. Industrial psychologists have investigated the effect of variety music, sweet music, classical music, waltzes, and rock music on production in factories and businesses. The same goes for illumination and its relation to work. Daylight, for example, has been demonstrated to provide the "best" illumination for work.

What kind of sound and lighting is best for play? Thanks to the people who filled out our questionnaires, we know that dim lighting and soft music are conducive to good afterplay:

I like dim lighting and red lights for atmosphere because it makes it so much more cozy and intimate. Atmosphere is so important. It kind of creates a mood. Your surroundings can make you feel sexier and if you feel sexy, you can do anything. (woman, 30)

I like a dark room, but with enough light to see each other (maybe candle light), and some music softly playing in the background. (man, 21)

I love to listen to very soft and romantic music (woman, 24)

Low music in the background, soft love music, with just one candle burning. (woman, 25)

I like candlelight, drenched with some jazz coming over the stereo. (man, 26)

I would like a low light so that we can see each other. (woman, 29)

A dim light, like a candle, maintains the mood, but I like to be able to see her. Looking at each other in such lighting and realizing that you really had each other feels wonderful. (man, 28)

I love to look at her hair and nipples in the flickering light and watch her looking at me. I sometimes can't believe it's happening. (man, 36)

I love to pull clean soft sheets over our bodies. I like candles of the orange or red spectrum of light, with soft jazz still playing—no intrusions or loud noises. (woman, 28)

I like seeing our bodies together in dim light. I like to be looked at tenderly—it makes me feel beautiful. (woman, 23)

Listening to music, we found, is a fairly popular afterplay activity. It also seems to be a frequent part of good or desired afterplay. Forty-two people specifically mentioned listening to music as an element in their ideal postintercourse experience. Most often, however, the listening itself is passive rather than active. Music can provide a kind of backdrop for the touching and talking that goes on between two lovers. It can also be conducive to conversation and sharing and may even help to stimulate such activity. But people certainly do not want to feel distracted or intruded upon by music.

Similarly, a particular type of nonintrusive lighting seems to provide the right kind of atmosphere for good afterplay. Thirty-six people mentioned dim lighting (red lights and especially candles were often mentioned) as part of their ideal experience. Seeing the partner in this intimate illumination seems to be highly desirable, more so than total darkness. Interestingly, most people who mentioned this kind of lighting also mentioned soft music.

We suggest that you experiment with lights and music after sex. It only takes a few moments to light a candle or to play a favorite record. A certain amount of forethought, of course, makes good sense. It wouldn't do to spend fifteen minutes looking for a favorite record—or a candle and matches—right after lovemaking.

Different Surroundings

Some people described particular romantic surroundings as part of their ideal postintercourse atmosphere. For most of us these would provide unusual environments for afterplay. But with afterplay, as with foreplay and intercourse, variety can be invigorating:

Once I was in a small cabin. The cabin was under some large trees in a garden. After we made love we could see the light streaming through stained glass windows and listen to the rustle of the trees. It was ideal. (woman, 30)

I would love to be by a fireplace, the coals just flickering lightly, with the sounds of water, ocean or brook in the background. (woman, 24)

After sex my favorite thing to do is look in each other's eyes, in front of a fireplace, at night, on a carpet with pillows all around. It is important that there be enough warmth from the fire so our nakedness isn't uncomfortable. (woman, 22)

My ideal afterplay is laying on a waterbed with moonlight and balmy spring air or maybe even a good old electrical storm. (woman, 26)

In the spring the ideal would be to simply listen to the birds and insects after making love in a newly sown field. (woman, 22)

It's nice to have ambiance, a warm comfortable bed, a fire, rain on the window, or sunshine, city lights and the like. (woman, 26)

The atmosphere perhaps could be some field of European flowers in the bright sun. Some vast and wide outdoor environment. (man, 20)

A number of people remarked that these unusual or beautiful surroundings for afterplay, however desirable, were unrealistic. Good afterplay certainly doesn't have to take place in a newly sown field, but why not try it—even once?

Our parents, teachers, and jobs ensure that most of us learn how to work. But in the process, too many of us over the years unlearn how to play. Others of us seem to know what we want in afterplay, but are too busy or too tired to act on our desires. As one woman said, "Unfortunately, this (my ideal afterplay) is rarely possible except on vacations or on rare days when we're off together."

We question the priorities that make everything else more important than ourselves. Weekend vacations are within the means of most of us and can provide the different, deroutinizing environments conducive to good afterplay. As a 24-year-old librarian said, "Being together wherever you have made love is ok. But an unusual and striking environment makes it special. The atmosphere is most important, that's why vacations help." Vacations and new surroundings help to break down patterned or dull ways of experiencing the world and each other. They deserve priority from time to time.

Of course even without new surroundings, without leaving home, you can treat yourself to the mini-vacation that good afterplay itself can provide. Real vacations are a fine idea, but the most important aspects of good afterplay—touching and talking—can happen anywhere.

Bathing

Water, aside from its cleansing and life-sustaining properties, feels good. For many people, water is relaxing, soothing, refreshing, or even healing. Splashing, swimming, and soaking have always been popular recreational activities. Many joggers say that the best part about running is relaxing in the shower afterward. Water is used in the rituals of many cultures to mark the passage from one state or activity to another. In baptism, for example, water is involved in the process of becoming Christian. We often bathe or shower as we go from waking up into day, or from the day's activities into sleep. Bathing as afterplay can also serve to help us make the gradual transition from a sexual consciousness to a more usual state of mind.

Anthropologists have noted that mutual grooming among primates (monkeys, great apes, and prosimians), is more than simply hygienic: It serves to establish and strengthen the social bonds of the group. Washing, bathing and showering together after sex may also serve to establish and sustain a relationship between two people. When we wash someone we are providing a most basic, intimate and humble service. We are also likely to be providing an expression of love and affection.

It's definitely a fantasy, but I'd love a jacuzzi at the foot of the bed, or a sauna nearby. (woman, 28)

The ideal experience would be a cold ocean to plunge into in the summer where I could revitalize my energy and make love again in the water with my lover. (woman, 22)

I'd love to jump into a pool. (woman, 22)

My ideal situation is to shower with my partner and then start making love again. (man, 35)

We have no plumbing, thus we miss the available water things, i.e., a wonderfully hot tub after sex. (man, 32)

I like to shower with my lover. We soap each other up and softly wash each other from head to toe. I love to kneel down and wash his legs, ass, and gently wash his penis. (woman, 31)

Although a number of people (22) mentioned showering or bathing with a partner as an aspect of their ideal afterplay, we must point out that some people said they would *not* enjoy washing up or bathing after sex—with or without their partners. For these people, there seems to be something especially close and friendly about *not* washing up together after intercourse. As Gabriel puts it in Thomas Hardy's novel *Far From the Madding Crowd,* "I never fuss about dirt in its pure state and when I know what sort it is. . . ."[9]

Lying together just the way you are may be fine afterplay—*if this is what you both want.* What is clearly not good afterplay is one person's abruptly going off to bathe or shower while the other lies alone in bed wondering why his or her partner *had* to go and clean up. If you have different preferences you might alternate between washing up and not washing up. But don't assume that the bather is compulsively clean, trying to rid himself of you—or that the non-bather is dirty. As long as the activities are shared they both have their appeal.

Food and Drink

What we eat and drink is very much determined by our culture and the process of socialization. We also come to learn that certain foods and drinks are appropriate for certain meals or time of day (cereals for breakfast, sandwiches for lunch, and so on). We were not surprised to find that many people enjoy eating and drinking after sex. But we were somewhat surprised to find that there seems to be a consensus as to the most desirable things to eat and drink during afterplay.

By far the most frequently desired afterplay beverage is wine. In America, people do not drink wine primarily to quench thirst. It is more often sipped, savored, enjoyed for its sensual quality—which makes it particularly suitable as a choice of drink during afterplay. Fruit and fruit juices were also frequently mentioned by our respondents. Other natural and basic food and drink were also mentioned by people as part of good afterplay.

The best thing that could possibly happen would be for a friend or servant to bring in a bowl of fresh fruit and water or drink. (woman, 28)

A big bowl of strawberries and watermelon or some wine. (man, 26)

I would like an opulent feast served by someone. I would like to share eating and drinking with him from the same plate and glass. (woman, 41)

Sometimes I would like to have my partner bring me strawberries and cream. (woman, 34)

I like a glass of wine. Although sex can have a pretty soporific effect on me, I can imagine being energized and wanting to go out to the park for a picnic. (woman, 26)

A bottle of wine, we share one glass. Some bread, cheese, fruit to nibble, we share with each other, feeding each other. (woman, 23)

After sex, the only thing I love to eat (excepting my partner, of course) are quiet and juicy fruits—pears, peaches, and plums. Sometimes fruit and nuts are nice, too. (man, 25)

Something cold to drink is heaven. (woman, 40)

I'm usually thirsty after intercourse. I enjoy drinking some cold juice. (woman, 25)

For 27 of our respondents, something to drink was a part of their ideal afterplay; for 17, something to eat. Wine, ice water, and fruit juices were the most frequently mentioned drinks, and the favorite afterplay food seems to be fruit—described as juicy or sensual by more than one person. It's interesting to note that no one mentioned soda, diet soda, or junk food as part of their ideal afterplay. Afterplay seems to require more natural nourishment.

The sharing of the same food and drink is an important aspect of many rituals and is an element of good afterplay. Drinking and eating from the same glass and plate seem to be a special and symbolic activity for some lovers. As in the Jewish marriage ceremony, during which wine is drunk from the same cup, the ingesting of the same substance can join two people—both physically and psychically.

What accounts for the discrepancy between the number of people who theoretically find food and drink highly desirable during afterplay, and the smaller percentage of people who actually enjoy these pleasures? Concern with weight can hardly be the answer; there are just not that many calories in small amounts of wine or fruit, and none in ice water. If intercourse is the last possible activity before sleeping, any active form of afterplay is ruled out. What is needed for eating and drinking, as for any form of afterplay, is time, awareness, and sensitivity. And once again, the material requirements are easy to find and inexpensive. If you keep a bottle of wine or a bowl of fruit or some water in the refrigerator, all you will need is one glass or one plate—and some good feelings.

Eating and drinking are, of course, only *aspects* of what people consider to be ideal afterplay. Few people mentioned only fruit or wine, lights or massage or any one thing, because afterplay is made up of a combination of atmosphere, activity, and feeling. If two people love each other and are interested in sharing themselves and their activities, the afterplay will be good for both of them.

The activities vary and I feel are not as important as the mood and feelings are. (man, 44)

It doesn't matter what my partner says. "The plants need watering." "Let's eat spaghetti." or "It really feels good being inside you." What matters is the way whatever is said is said tenderly and honestly. (woman, 24)

Whatever we do, it is the good warm feeling in us and between us that is there. (woman, 35)

In the reports that follow, we can see the extent to which both men and women view ideal afterplay as a whole experience rather than one simply made up of its parts.

Men

A 21-year-old student who has been going out with a female student for three years says:

> To feel as one with my partner would be the ideal thing for me. At least the feeling of transcending the individual being so that we both derive the joy of being united through the act of making love. What we say and do should fall into place naturally. Sometimes I am into the afterglow of caressing and talking. It is the sharing of an experience that is the ideal thing for me.

Another 21-year-old student, who has been going out with a 19-year-old, knows what he would like his partner to say:

> That she is feeling really good, secure, warm, together—and that she wants to remain in my company for a long while. Drugs such as pot or coke might be a good idea followed by oral sex. This would be called "the total burn-to-exhaustion scenario." An alternative might be on some occasions to work together on some project (something fun and creative, like playing music and singing for awhile). Sometimes the implications of intercourse and the development of the relationship come to mind. Sometimes it is a beautiful time and no words need to be spoken. It can be a period of silent understanding.

A 26-year-old man who has been living with a 27-year-old woman for three years says that for his ideal afterplay:

> I would like a quiet environment—no noise from the outside. A late sunny afternoon, or night with candles burning. Some

soft jazz on the stereo. A big bowl of strawberries and watermelon. Wine. French cigarettes. From my partner I would like touching and caressing and gentle conversation about our lovemaking or our relationship in general. Afterwards I'd like to take a sauna.

A 37-year-old professional married one year says:

I like a drink of juice or water (blood sugar condition), nasal spray and/or a handkerchief (sinuses), a cooling off period (though I want to keep touching her, too). This is what being a basket case means. I also like soft light, rock on the radio, a visit from the cat, talking about ourselves and all our tomorrows. She already does what I love: her inner quiet and tranquility counterbalance my high. Her chuckling at my carryings-on makes me feel I'm on a stage. We laugh a lot and touch a lot. Most important, we feel so incredibly *close* to each other.

A consultant, 60 years old, has been married for 14 years. He says:

I like to snuggle up to my partner. I want to be warm and tender to her. I like to feel she thought I was the greatest. I like half-light. I like to be able to see her. I love to feel she gets the same pleasure I do when I arouse her and finally help her to have an orgasm.

Women

A 30-year-old secretary from a large metropolitan area says:

The best experience is to be in love with your partner and to realize that you have been able to express that to your partner. The atmosphere can vary. Maybe quiet and peaceful, subdued lighting, some music, maybe something to eat or drink—cool. I would like him to say anything sincerely caring that doesn't ring of neurosis or dependency. I like him to sound calm, content, appreciative of things, with a lack of fear. But the best times are tactile and words come haltingly and are unnecessary. Any activity, even jumping out of bed, could be done with love or hate. It is the attitude that counts. Lovemaking is the greatest improvisation—a dance of life and few people can understand what it's all about.

A computer programmer in her mid-20s who has been married for six years likes to be:

in the bedroom holding each other, sharing something to eat (of course in the nude). I would like him to tell me how beautiful I am and how great in bed he thinks I am. I would want him to kiss me and touch me all over and maybe start over again.

A student, 19 years old and not living with her 20-year-old boyfriend, wrote:

I find it ideal to be told that I am beautiful, a great lover and am loved. I like dim lighting so that I can see my partner and like the window slightly open. Relaxing music and clean sheets are always nice. I also very much like to have my cat in bed after intercourse. I seem to be highly attached to the furry thing and love his body against mine. I also *love* to have my breasts caressed. I love to hold my partner after sex. The conversation after sex is also always very comforting.

A 22-year-old graduate student who has been living with a man for two years says her ideal afterplay is to have her partner stay inside her for a while,

holding me lightly and caressing me, playing with my hair. Me doing the same to him. Talking and laughing a lot, telling each other we love one another and how nice it feels to be joined together as we are. I like sun streaming in the room and something to munch on within reach so we can feed each other. I like soft music in the background.

A 25-year-old secretary from the east coast, married five years, says:

Ideally I'd like to lounge around for a bit, verbalizing my usual feelings of romance and well being. I'd like to shower together in a dimly lit bathroom, with music in the background. Perhaps go out for a romantic dinner someplace "different," or maybe just lay around, building up energy for another more subdued session. I love the idea of champagne and candle atmosphere for the before, during, and after feelings. Because I'm so eager to express my feelings, I'd enjoy my partner's doing the same. Because I feel communication is so important to any relationship, I attribute a good deal of importance to communication about sex. I do feel that postintercourse communication—be it eye contact, hand holding, laughing, or talking—is an essential ingredient to a healthy sexual relationship.

A 31-year-old mother of three described her ideal afterplay as being

close to my partner—to remain joined with caressing and talking. A massage within one-half hour after intercourse followed by more intercourse wouldn't be bad either with someone who really turns me on, followed by the maid bringing in cool tall drinks.

A 24-year-old nurse who has been seeing a man for four years says:

I enjoy making love on the floor in front of the fire—after which I would prefer to bundle up and talk for hours or go and look at the stars. I prefer no one else in the house (there is usually a seven-year-old lurking somewhere). I would like my partner to tell me he loves me, sometimes he does. I would like him to caress my face and body and kiss me—often.

A 32-year-old mother and teacher has been seeing a lawyer for four years, although they are both married to different people. She says:

If we always had the situation of living together I would never want to give up the quietude and warmth of our postintercourse touching and conversation. It is nicest to have light rather than total darkness at night and the enjoyment of a long time (one half-hour to an hour) to slowly reenter daily living or decide to sleep cuddled together. In the morning if we have to go to work, I love the moments of pleasurable holding followed by a generally silent morning preparation—one of us makes coffee, while the other makes the bed, sharing a shower or bath, shaving, brushing teeth and as time goes on more conversation over breakfast. I love a slowness of voice and movement for a long time after intercourse, whether it is in lying together in bed preparing for sleep or beginning a day with relaxation. My ideal after-intercourse experience is in the morning with a whole free day ahead—making love, talking and holding. I always fall back to sleep and my partner makes coffee and reads. Then he rejoins me in bed, sometimes for a second lovemaking, sometimes for holding and slow awakening to the smell of fresh coffee and a warm smiling face.

CHAPTER 6

What People
Don't Like

When we asked people what they did not want to have
happen after sex, the replies often showed anger, disappointment or sadness. A woman in her 30s mentioned "being rushed
or put aside in order to go on to another activity." A man in his
late 20s objected to his partner's rushing into the bathroom to
wash up, or saying, "What a mess." And a woman of 19 spoke
for many women (and not a few men) of all ages when she said,
"What I hate most after sex is when my partner feels compelled
to rationalize what took place. Specifically, when he starts
explaining how what happened shouldn't be taken seriously."
Most of us would agree with her implicit assertion that sex is
serious—not serious in the sense of being somber or solemn, but
in the sense of being important or significant.

Many people worry about "breaking the mood" before sex
begins; we believe that it is even more important not to break
the mood *after* lovemaking.

More women than men described negative postintercourse experiences, and in greater detail. Women have more often been the victims of thoughtless afterplay than men. But a sizable number of men mentioned the same negative experiences as women, such as immediate sleep by the partner, lack of attention, and mundane conversation. In any case, the attitude that "I'm content. If my partner isn't, that's her (his) problem" is ultimately self-defeating. When one half of a couple is unhappy, the couple is unhappy.

Bursting the Bubble: When Sharing Ends

When sex goes very well, when you and your partner enjoy foreplay and intercourse and you both experience orgasm, you might say that you have shared a delightful experience. But, paradoxically, at just that moment when things were most delightful (orgasm), you may have not been sharing at all. For some people, as they become more and more aroused it may be more and more difficult for them to think of anything but how good they themselves feel.

After intercourse and orgasm, however, you can experience a kind of sharing which is transcendent. This kind of sharing is very much like a bubble blown by a child—it is beautiful and may rise high, but it is fleeting and, most of all, fragile. Time and again, when people described negative postcoital experiences they were describing words, actions, or occurrences that burst the bubble, that ended the sharing.

We will soon see how easy it is to break the mood of good afterplay by what we say. There are, in addition, a number of things people do—along with things that "happen"—that can just as easily spoil your afterplay. We have put the word "happen" in quotes because we do not believe that there are very many things in life that just happen. Much of the time, with just a little foresight, we can make sure certain things *don't* happen. For example, many people said that having the phone ring during afterplay was a turn-off. Think about it. Isn't there a very easy way to make sure this doesn't "happen"?

Most of us fail to realize just how much control we have over what "happens" to us.

Sleeping

Consider sleep. We talk of how we "fall asleep," as if sleep somehow and mysteriously takes us over. Many aspects of sleep are mysterious, but there is nothing mysterious about when it is likely to occur. If you get up at 7:00 A.M. and you work, you will probably begin to feel sleepy by 11:00 P.M. It is no coincidence that this is the hour at which television prime time comes abruptly to an end.

As we saw in Chapter 3, sleep is a very common postintercourse behavior. A majority of Americans go to sleep within an hour after sex, and a large proportion often go to sleep directly after (in our study, the proportion was approximately one-third). What makes this a subject for concern is the fact that so many people cited the partner's going directly to sleep as a negative postintercourse experience. (The only thing mentioned more often was the partner's *physically* leaving.) More than one woman in three specifically mentioned her partner's going directly to sleep as a negative experience:

When my partner falls asleep, it's an insult to me. (woman, 27)

If the man falls asleep immediately after sex without holding me or touching me in any way, I feel rejected and hurt. (woman, 23)

Fall asleep and say absolutely nothing. (woman, 21)

I do not like my partner to just turn over and go to sleep without some sort of verbal or physical acknowledgment of a shared pleasant experience. (woman, 23)

It's a negative experience to have my partner immediately roll over and fall asleep. That is ignoring me and the fact that we'd just shared what I consider a very important aspect of the relationship. (woman, 26)

Turning away from me to sleep. Falling asleep and not having his arm around me. (woman, 25)

I especially don't like people who go to sleep. (woman, 24)

A sizable number of men also mentioned the partner's going to sleep as something they did not or would not like:

I also don't like my partner to pull away and go to sleep. (man, 23)

I would not like my partner to quickly withdraw and turn away from me and fall immediately to sleep without a word. (man, 63)

If my partner were to fall asleep immediately I think it would leave an empty feeling within me. (man, 21)

Any man who has had the experience of his partner's going directly to sleep when *he* is wide awake and ready for talking and continued touching, knows that this is indeed a negative experience. Those men who regularly fall asleep on their partners immediately after intercourse should try to imagine how they would feel if this were done to them on a regular basis.

How can you make it more likely that you will stay awake right after sex? A very simple step is to begin lovemaking a little earlier than you usually do. If you have fairly set habits, don't try radical changes: if you customarily begin foreplay at around a quarter to 11, try starting one night at 10:15 or 10:30. You should find yourself a little less sleepy when intercourse is complete. On occasion you might plan your day so you'll feel more energetic after sex. Why not take a nap or give yourself a relaxing break? Perhaps one reason we're so sleepy after sex is because we overfill our days to the point that being dead tired in the evening is practically inevitable.

You will certainly find yourself less tired out after sex if you are in good physical condition. That means eating well, and it means exercising. Some runners report that they sleep more soundly and need less sleep than they did before starting a running program. There are also indications that exercise directly benefits the sexual experience, and given the physiological stress of sex, it makes sense that the physically fit body will enjoy it more and be less exhausted by it. We wonder if this isn't a major motivation behind the current craze for jogging.

Perhaps, on nights when you are really tired, you should think twice about having sex. A 32-year-old woman wrote of her partner, "Would not like him to just roll over and go to sleep (which, fortunately *he's* never done). He has enough sense to say he's tired ahead of time." And he has earned his fatigue. He is a construction worker and he is 52 years old.

Physically Leaving

You don't have to go to sleep in order to end the sharing that constitutes good afterplay. You can always actually leave.

If you do, you're likely to be setting in motion the most painful postcoital experience of all, often for both partners. The reality of a partner's leaving is, of course, more frequent when the couple does not live together. In fact, one of the many joys of living with someone is that you don't have to worry about getting home after sex; you are home.

How painful leave-taking can be is described beautifully in Mary Gordon's novel, *Final Payments*. Isabel stays awake through the sleep of her married lover:

He slept for two hours holding my head down on his chest with one hand to keep me there. I couldn't sleep. My eyes were wide in the dark; I could pick out the yellow flowers in my curtains, but the red ones had disappeared. I felt joy and fear, breathing in the dark hairs of his chest and then remembering that when he woke he would be leaving. I had to lie perfectly still; the moment he awoke he would already have left me.[1]

In their descriptions of negative afterplay experiences, more people mentioned their partner's leaving quickly than anything else. Women:

The most negative after-intercourse experience I can think of would be to have my partner immediately get up, get dressed and leave the room or apartment to do whatever. (woman, 25)

I would not like my partner to immediately get up with a "that's that" attitude. (woman, 33)

A man getting up, putting on his clothes and going home— especially to his wife. (woman, 30)

If my partner left abruptly to go somewhere. (woman, 31)

I would feel hurt and angry if my partner had no interest in being with me directly after intercourse. (woman, 23)

And men (the first, a homosexual):

When the other person gets dressed, is up and out. Not that sexually I haven't been satisfied, but I expect more from people in general. (man, 24)

Abrupt departure of my partner. (man, 24)

I would not like her to get up and go away. (man, 25)

Getting up and leaving right afterwards. (man, 23)

If my partner were to want to leave, I think it would leave an empty feeling within me. (man, 21)

Another 21-year-old man was the only respondent who commented on the problems of the one who is leaving:

Another negative experience is having to leave right away—makes one feel like "Wham bam thank you ma'am."

If ever there is a time that people should and usually do want to stay together, it is after sex. And generally, remaining together is possible. The classic exception, of course, is the affair, in which leave-taking is so often painful. How then can affairs flourish at all if this most unpleasant of postintercourse behaviors is a regular occurrence? The answer involves what happens between sex and leave-taking. If the afterplay is long and intimate, the affair is likely to continue and possibly threaten the primary relationship. If afterplay is brief and impersonal, the affair is less likely to last.

An example is the case of Stan C.

Drinking beer and smoking cigarettes

Stan C., a 30-year-old graduate student, has been living with an elementary school teacher for two years. During this time he has been involved in a number of other sexual relationships, although he has always tried to keep these involvements hidden from the woman with whom he lives. Stan says he is happy with all aspects of his sexual relationship with her. They have sex about two or three times per week and they typically share some compliments and kindness afterwards. After a few more minutes of hugging or chatting, Stan usually begins to think about his classes or some other upcoming activity.

When Stan has sex with another woman, the postcoital period is quite different: "If I am in my own apartment I have to worry about how to get her out before my girlfriend gets home. If I've enjoyed myself I try not to be too blatant in my actions so as to induce her to return. I usually feel a bit apprehensive. If I am at her place I worry about how I can get home gracefully without spending the night and still be invited back."

There are other things Stan would not like to have happen during the postintercourse period besides having his girlfriend walk in right after he has had an orgasm. He hates to hear the words, "Why did you come so quick?" or "I prefer my girlfriend." He also finds it repulsive if a lover "takes a shower, relieves herself without closing the bathroom door, or bleeds on the sheets."

If one of Stan's partners fails to reach an orgasm, his response varies greatly. If he doesn't plan to see the woman again, he does nothing. If he does plan to see her again, "I try to make some nonthreatening inquiries that might enable her to avoid a similar problem next time." If the woman complains or "makes a scene," Stan will usually tell her to either "fuck off or buy a vibrator."

Of course, there are times when the postintercourse period is much more pleasant for Stan. He likes to sit up in bed, drinking beer and smoking cigarettes while chatting about past sexual and emotional involvements. Stan is very precise about what he would most like to hear his partner say in the postcoital period. The words would go something like this: "Listen, I know you have a girlfriend, and I don't give a damn—we can still get together comfortably once a week or so—we're both mature people."

Physically leaving and falling asleep are just two of the ways we can leave our partners after sex. There are others that may be equally, if not more, hurtful to a relationship.

Ignoring Your Partner

Although we appreciated those respondents who wrote at length in their essays, sometimes a very short response was as enlightening as a long one. An example of this was the 25-year-old woman whose entire answer to Question 42 was two words: "Being ignored." In one way or another, many respondents said that this would be (or had been, or was) a negative postintercourse experience. Sometimes, ignoring and sleeping were linked.

I would not like my partner to fall asleep or in any way show boredom or intense distraction or absence of mind. (man, 20)

To be ignored or to make me feel unimportant. (woman, 33)

A negative experience is when the partner turns his back and falls asleep. Or when he doesn't say anything. (woman, 23)

I would not like my partner to turn his back to me and simply "forget" the lovemaking act we'd just shared. Another negative experience for me would occur if my partner would refuse my physical contact or gestures of affection by pushing me away or by simply moving to another bed or leaving the room entirely and not returning to my side. If any of these situations would occur after making love, I'd conclude that the act had been one of only physical gratification for my partner, devoid of emotion. (woman, 27)

I wouldn't like it if my partner didn't want to touch me. I wouldn't like it if my partner didn't want to talk and be kind to me or if he wanted to get up out of bed to do something else. In short, I feel emotionally very close to my partner after sex. If I or my partner didn't feel this, or didn't convey this, then I would be dissatisfied. (woman, 22)

My partner's swift departure, either by refusing to touch or be close or refusing to talk or communicate. (woman, 22)

Coldness, remoteness, nontouching. (man, 53)

I would not like it if he did not hold me or express some feeling. I guess what I would not like most is him saying or doing nothing at all. *(woman, 28)*

Most descriptions of being ignored implied that the withdrawal of both verbal and physical attention was involved. But some respondents emphasized one or the other. The verbal:

If it's with a partner I care for and think that she feels the same, I would feel hurt if there were no special shared communication afterwards. (man, 30)

Not responding verbally, no expression of satisfaction. (woman, 26)

I would dislike it if my partner said nothing. (woman, 27)

And the physical:

Having me not wanting to hold her. (man, 60)

Not holding me. (woman, 25)

I would not like a sharp break in contact. The continuation of physical contact is crucial after intercourse . . . I need time to be slowly weaned from the physical experience and would not want to be pushed away or ignored immediately after intercourse. (woman, 27)

As was often the case, the feelings of many people were summarized by a very young woman. This time it was a 19-year-old California student, who wrote, "I also don't like the 'if-we're-finished-why-should-we-still-hold-each-other' attitude. Sex, for me, brings out a lot of feelings, not only sexual, and they can't be turned off and denied because we've 'stopped.'" She has put the word *stopped* in quotation marks—which is exactly where it belongs, since the sexual encounter does not end at orgasm.

It was clear that fewer men than women had ever actually

suffered the experience of a partner who ignored them after sex, but the quotes from men do indicate that many of them are at least aware of how hurtful it can be. And the responses of some men indicate that when these particular tables are turned, the experience is most unpleasant. One 26-year-old man was blunt about it: "Bummers are partners who want to separate quick."

While the solution to this problem seems obvious, it may not be so simple. Habits are hard to break, and men especially may find postcoital intimacy difficult at first. But since it is so important, we strongly advise trying. If, at first, you feel uncomfortable with full body contact, try stroking your partner or holding hands. If romantic words do not come easily, try talking about almost any comfortable topic. Many people like to talk about *themselves*, and your partner is likely to enjoy this, too. An 18-year-old woman did not like her partner to talk about "other rambling things," but would not at all mind hearing "about him or how he's feeling." As we will see shortly, a little caution is in order here; for example, putting yourself down, talking about your problems, or, most important talking about other partners is not advisable. But if you just "think positive," there is a good chance that almost anything you say will be appreciated by your partner.

Rushing (To Work or Other Activity)

A major theme that emerged from our research is that couples enjoy themselves more if they *take time* for sex, allowing themselves ample time for all the phases of the sexual encounter. Nowhere is this theme echoed more clearly than in those responses that specifically mention rushing or its equivalent. Rushing is rarely pleasant (do we enjoy rushing to catch a train or to get to a class on time?), but when we have to rush somewhere right after sex, the inherent unpleasantness of rushing is magnified by our "postcoital languor."

I dislike having to rush to get dressed to go out, etc. (woman, 30)

Rushing for an appointment, class, etc. . . . (quick movement) (woman, 21)

Having to rush out of the house to some matter of business. (woman, 28)

Having to get up and run somewhere right away. (man, 28)

Get right up and go to work. (man, 29)

Do not like to get out of bed and do something immediately—especially leaving the house and most especially going to work. (woman, 32)

I don't like to have to jump up immediately after intercourse to tend to chores. (woman, 34)

People also objected to their partners' having to rush off. A 34-year-old woman said she would dislike "being rushed or put aside in order to go on to another activity." And, as the following case shows, many men also savor the relaxed intimacy of afterplay and would dislike their partners' having to rush.

Time to relax, caress, talk

Bob S. is a 38-year-old electrician who lives in Maryland. His wife, who is several years younger than he, recently had a tubal ligation after the birth of their fourth child. In this decision, as in any important matter, they were open in discussion of their feelings. What has always attracted Bob to his wife is her "loving, giving, sensitive, and gentle" nature. They have been married for over 14 years and have known each other for 16.

Bob, happily married, greatly enjoys the sexual part of his marriage. He derives much pleasure from foreplay, which may sometimes last half an hour. He is also happy with intercourse and with its frequency, which is two or three times a week.

The postintercourse period is highly enjoyable to Bob, who considers it to be important. It is not a time for sleep, but rather "a time to relax, talk, caress." Praise is a frequent part of Bob's afterplay, both the giving and the receiving. Although like many people he eventually gets out of bed to wash up, he never does so without first experiencing some of the relaxing pleasures he describes.

In general Bob is a hard worker, but he values his leisure time. He exercises regularly, likes spending time with his family, and prefers his days off to be as unstructured as possible. Recreation of all kinds is to be fully enjoyed. One of the things he would not like after lovemaking would be his partner's "having to rush to another appointment, abruptly 'turning me off.'"

If you are in the habit of having sex just before you go to work or to some other chore, try it at a different time. The feeling of not having to be somewhere is almost always pleasant; after sex it can be delightful.

Singular Activities

In the previous chapter we showed that certain activities, such as bathing, could be part of ideal afterplay, provided that both partners wanted the activity. Similarly, not cleaning off could be ideal, if both partners enjoyed staying in bed as is. Problems may develop if you like to do one thing after sex and your partner prefers to do something else. The following activities were mentioned by several people as part of their ideal afterplay, but by a greater number of people as negative experiences. Since this was true in each case—more people called them negative than positive—we suggest that if you are the one who likes the activity, try *not* doing it for a time or two.

Getting Up to Wash

There are many people who do not like to wash up after sex and who find it unpleasant when their partner does so.

I would not like my partner to go in and wash himself off after sex. (woman, 23)

I used to have a partner who got up almost immediately after intercourse to wash himself off—yech, terrible for the "mood"—and my ego. (woman, 24)

Having partner get up and shower immediately. Definitely a turn-off. (woman, 25)

Partner rushes to bathroom to wash up or says, "What a mess." (man, 28)

When my partner gets up right away and washes off I feel that he wants to rid himself of me as quickly as possible. (woman, 34)

The woman jumping up immediately to "clean" herself off, i.e., to remove any trace of lovemaking. (man, 33)

If the man got up immediately to wash his penis or legs or hands or mouth. (woman, 23)

Women, supposedly the more squeamish sex, seem more comfortable than men with the secretions of sex. And physically, of course, there is nothing to be uncomfortable about. Saliva, vaginal secretions, and seminal fluid are nonpoisonous, harmless, and—to some—true sources of sensual delight.

The quotes show that what troubles people is not the washing so much as the timing (the words "immediately," "right away," and "rush" showed up frequently in the descriptions). If you do enjoy washing off, how about a joint bath or shower? Washing or cleaning when you do it together and take your time doing it, can be highly enjoyable after sex.

Another solution is to keep a towel or tissues next to the bed. A number of people mentioned that they cleaned themselves with a towel after sex. While this may not altogether please your partner (it still "removes the traces of lovemaking"), you at least avoid leaving his or her side.

Reading and Watching Television

Reading and watching television are common postintercourse activities for many Americans, television being the more popular of the two. Both activities are enjoyable, and neither will break the mood the way a critical remark will—especially if there is a period of time between intercourse and these activities. Still, they are not truly shared (television is more so than reading, unless one partner reads to the other). In fact, either activity can be viewed as an attempt to escape intimacy. Of those who mentioned TV or reading as negative activities after sex, nearly all were women:

I don't want him to ignore me and watch TV. (woman, 17)

I'd be angry if he left me right away to watch television or read. (woman, 40)

Having partner get up and leave, especially to watch TV (very tacky). (woman, 25)

I would not like him turning on the TV or reading a book, unless I wanted to do those things, too. (woman, 26)

The last quote shows that watching television or reading can be welcome as afterplay if both partners enjoy doing them. But when only one of you wants to read or watch, you have a problem similar to that described in the case of washing or cleaning up. Our suggestions are similar, too. If you are the reader or watcher, and your partner would prefer you not to be, try going along with him or her once. If it is really a habit, see if you can hold off for a while after sex. Leave your book unopened 15 minutes longer than you usually do. Or, if you typically finish intercourse a short while before your favorite program, why not start your next sexual encounter somewhat earlier than usual?

Smoking

Quite aside from its being dangerous to health, smoking is undermining to satisfactory afterplay. And from the responses we received, it appears that this is one after-sex activity experienced as negative by at least as many men as women:

I really don't like her smoking. (man, 28)

Smoking (which he doesn't do) in bed annoys me. (woman, 27)

Simply, I do dislike her smoking habits, particularly in bed and after intercourse. (man, 35)

It's easy to see why smoking is often considered disagreeable after sex. The smoke itself is distracting—and, for many people, distinctly unpleasant. More important, it is awkward to touch and impossible or dangerous to kiss your partner while he or she is smoking, and the smell may make a kiss unpleasant after the cigarette is put out.

Interruptions

In describing the ideal afterplay experience, our respondents often mentioned privacy and quiet. Anything which disturbs this atmosphere is likely to break the mood of afterplay, a mood which is difficult if not impossible to reestablish. You and your partner are holding each other, loving each other, feeling good, laughing together—and suddenly the phone rings, or there is a knock on the door, or one of your children rushes into the room. Your bubble has been burst.

These were, in fact, the three kinds of interruptions cited most often by respondents. Men and women seem to be equally disturbed by them:

Having the mood cut short by a phone call or fussy child would surely be negative. (woman, 29)

If people came over and we couldn't be alone. (woman, 18)

Telephone ringing, knock on the door. (man, 28)

The phone ringing, people dropping by unexpectedly, i.e., being interrupted. (man, 26)

After I have a fulfilling experience, I would not like my son to wake up immediately afterwards expecting to be changed and bottle fed. I need time to relax and rest. (woman, 26)

To be interrupted by the children, phone, or visitors. (woman, 32)

Anything which would cause too sudden a change in mood or tempo. A ringing telephone is an external offense. (man, 50)

In *Pulling Your Own Strings*, Wayne Dyer lists a series of problems and then gives the "victim" response and the "nonvictim" response. One of these scenarios features a telephone ringing while you are in the middle of sex. A victim response, says Dyer, is to answer the phone; a nonvictim response is to let it ring.[2]

But as far as afterplay is concerned, and, we suspect, the preceding phases as well, both of the above could be considered victim responses. Even if you do not answer the phone, the ring itself is jarring. We suggest, therefore, that before you begin lovemaking you either bury the telephone or take the receiver off the hook. (If you take the receiver off, no noise will come from the phone if you turn the dial and insert a pencil to keep the dial from returning to "neutral.") Not only will you have saved yourself from this all-too-common disturbance, but, as one man pointed out to us, you will have saved the caller from potential embarrassment.

My wife and I had just completed intercourse. It was about 10:30 P.M. and we were lying together feeling very good and loving. Suddenly the phone rang. I picked it up and it was a woman who my wife knows, although not very well. The caller could tell immediately that she had chosen a bad time, especially when she heard my wife cursing in the background. Of course, it ruined our afterplay, but I think it was worse for the caller.

The unexpected visitor can also ruin your afterplay, even if you do not answer the door. It is probably impossible to make certain this never happens, but you can lower the likelihood. Next time a friend drops by at an hour when you might logically be having sex, let him or her know that in the future you would appreciate a call first. Although this request may seem overly formal to you, it can prevent the kind of embarrassment which may simultaneously weaken a friendship and a sexual relationship. If you are the one planning the visit, and you get a busy signal, don't assume your friend is talking to someone on the phone, and don't visit unannounced.

Let's face it: Few parents are able to continue the kind of sexual spontaneity they enjoyed before having children. Nevertheless, planning your sexual encounter, and looking forward to it, can be highly enjoyable. With an infant in the house it may be impossible to avoid the occasional intrusion of a baby's crying (a sound that most adults simply cannot ignore), but by carefully scheduling your sexual encounters you can virtually guarantee yourself an hour or more of uninterrupted loving— including afterplay.

As for the older child, nature has ensured that parents can

normally have time for lovemaking at night: the typical child needs considerably more sleep than its parents. A five-year-old, for example, is likely to sleep 10 or 11 hours a night, which gives the typical couple 2 to 4 hours alone and awake. And as children get older, they spend more time out of the house (school, friends, etc.), thus giving you and your spouse additional time to play. Keep in mind that couples who spend some time away from their children have more, not less, to offer them as parents.

A few other interruptions were also mentioned: A 28-year-old woman told us that she and her partner were listening to music on the radio during the postintercourse period. Shortly the news came on with the typical lead story of death and destruction. "It broke the mood," she said. If you like music, you're better off listening to records or tapes than to a radio.

Having your partner's wife or husband walk in was mentioned as an interruption that is certain to ruin the atmosphere, as is having your own wife or husband walk in.

And two respondents described a leak in the waterbed as a negative postcoital experience!

The following were also mentioned in passing:

"Having to attend a bar-mitzvah or wedding;"
"Calling my broker;"
"Discussing death;"
"Having to hang up the clothes;"
"My partner telling me she is pregnant;"
"My partner telling me he has V.D.;" and
"My partner constantly talking about the book he is writing on afterplay!"

Did I Say Something Wrong?

A fool's mouth is his destruction.
—Biblical proverb

We saw in Chapter 3 that although a large number of people say little or nothing to their partner after intercourse, most people *do* talk to each other. In fact, of all the activities listed in Question 44, talking was the one most commonly checked off. Most of us expect and appreciate conversation after sex and are, at the very least, disappointed when it doesn't take place. One respondent admitted that it was very difficult for him to talk during the postintercourse period; he said he realized that this was not a good situation and he was trying to rectify it. However, it is not simply conversation that we want. There are certain kinds of conversation we particularly desire—the kind described in the preceding chapter. The right word or phrase can make afterplay a delight.

But every possibility of great joy carries with it the possibility of great unhappiness. Consider, for example, the atmosphere in the locker room of the team that has just won and the team that has just lost the seventh game of a World Series. Afterplay is no exception. The wrong word or phrase can make it a disaster.

What are the wrong things to say? Some are obvious. Many people mentioned them, and they came as no surprise. But other remarks, which may seem innocent, also have the potential for hurting your relationship.

Of course it isn't necessary to measure your words carefully in the postintercourse period. After all, you are in bed and not at a job interview. But, if you are in the habit of engaging in any of the kinds of postcoital conversation described below, you would do well to think before you speak.

Arguing

Couples fight. In fact, fighting with someone with whom you have been having a sexual relationship is itself a sign of growing intimacy. If you are now married to or living with someone, think back to the first few times you went out together. There was probably very little if any arguing. Only when you began to become close did occasional fights arise. In a sense, the first fight is more significant than the first lovemaking session.

Although research in social psychology shows that people with similar interests and attitudes are more likely to be attracted to one another than those whose interests are very different (that is, similars rather than opposites attract), no two people ever share exactly the same likes, dislikes, and needs. Which virtually guarantees that conflicts will arise in a relationship and that arguments will—or should—take place.

As James Leslie McCary points out in his excellent book, *Freedom and Growth in Marriage*, "marital conflict is patently inevitable." McCary goes on to say that couples who want to have a good marriage must therefore learn not to avoid conflict (one cannot avoid the inevitable), but to *manage* it. In his opinion the ways in which a couple learns to manage conflict "may be the most pivotal factor in their marriage."[3] Some years ago a book was published called *The Intimate Enemy*. It is, essentially, a handbook of marital conflict-management. Among the authors' (Dr. George R. Bach and Peter Wyden) suggestions was that spouses make appointments for their fights.[4] You and your partner may be reluctant to go that far, but you certainly can avoid fighting in the postintercourse period. As a 25-year-old man put it, "Getting into a fight after lovemaking is decidedly negative." An even stronger statement was made by a 33-year-old woman, whose entire answer to the question of what she would not like after sex consisted of two words: "An argument." The best explanation for *why* fighting is such bad afterplay came from a 27-year-old male homosexual, who said that "it would be unpleasant to get into an argument or revert to presex difficulties as though the sexual interlude was an aside." As we will see, anything which makes sex an "aside" makes afterplay negative.

How can you avoid fighting after sex? Simple. Avoid topics which are likely to lead to arguments. Perhaps you should make a mental list of taboo topics—things you have agreed not to talk about after intercourse. You might even write out the list and keep it next to your bed. If the postcoital conversation heads in the direction of one of those topics, even if the conversation seems pleasant, stop. Control yourself. It can wait for later. Things that can't wait usually will keep you from having sex in the first place.

Criticism

> To mourn a mischief that is past and gone
> Is the next way to draw new mischief on.
> —Shakespeare, *Othello*, Act I, Scene 3

Your list of topics to avoid will be unique, although we suspect that many lists will include "in-laws" and "money matters." But one, a particular type of verbal behavior, mentioned by a great many men and women, belongs on everyone's list: *Criticism*, especially when it involves the sexual act itself. To be criticized is rarely pleasant, even if the criticism is constructive and ultimately helpful. But in the postintercourse period, when your partner is likely to be needing affectionate or complimentary words, what he or she does not want to hear is, as one 27-year-old woman wrote, "Wow, what a lousy lover you are. Boy, was that a big disappointment!"

A number of other women mentioned critical comments:

You need to exercise the tops of your legs. (woman, 32)

You could have been better. You didn't move. (woman, 32)

You sure were dry. (woman, 34)

You can never do it right for me. (woman, 33)

You were better last night. (woman, 21)

A 22-year-old woman summed up the feelings of many when she wrote, "Any experience which is degrading is terrible—devastating in fact. Evaluations of performance and criticism of technique are demoralizing."

Men, of course, don't like to be criticized either. In fact, of all the negative behaviors—both verbal and nonverbal—mentioned by men, criticism was cited most often. Some specific comments listed as negative:

Would not like to be told I wasn't any good in bed. (man, 39)

To be put down for one's performance. (man, 41)

Being told it wasn't very good. (man, 28)

Partner tells me it was so-so or lousy sex. (man, 28)

If the woman started attacking the way I had sex or attacked me personally, that would put a damper on my mood. (man, 22)

Here is one of the rare situations where it may indeed be possible to avoid displeasing all of the people all of the time. *No one* likes to have their sexual "technique" criticized, especially not right after sex. It is likely to put a damper on anyone's mood. Does this mean you should be dishonest, that you should pretend everything was wonderful when it wasn't? No, but it does mean that any aspect of your partner's sexual behavior that you would like to see changed should be discussed some other time. In fact, you're probably better off talking about sexual problems before sex rather than after. If there is something you especially like or don't like during lovemaking, don't assume that your partner can guess what you want. With sensitivity and tact, express your feeling as to what he or she can do about it. And then avoid bringing it up again, at least unfavorably, until long after the sex itself is over.

The whole question of "performance" in bed is one of the major threats to good sexual relationships in our society today. Remember that like you, your partner is open and vulnerable after sex. As we shall see later in this chapter, many people dislike any discussion of sex as performance, but a negative rating is always painful. When lovemaking begins, both you and your partner should feel secure and comfortable in the knowledge that you will not be criticized after it is over.

Self-critical comments can also be very unwelcome afterplay. A man in his early 40s reported to us that, after a first lovemaking session with a very attractive woman, he experienced a quick let-down when the first thing she said was, "Now I'll probably never see you again." He told us that the sex itself was fine; that, until she made her comment, he was planning to continue the relationship. As it was, what she said became a self-fulfilling prophecy. Certainly the mood after sex is broken by comments like, "I wasn't too good, was I?" or "I'm so terribly sorry. I always have this problem." Afterplay is no place for self-deprecation, especially sexual self-deprecation.

Excessive Expressions of Affection

Because criticism is poor afterplay it does not automatically follow that romantic words are always good. They certainly can be, of course. People in the strongest relationships often exchange loving words, and many of our respondents listed such exchanges as a major component of ideal afterplay. But as almost all of us have found out at one time or another, a potentially good relationship can be stillborn because one of the partners was too romantic *too soon*.

Although a few women have told us that they were upset by men who expressed deep love after only one or two sexual encounters, the problem of excessive expressions of affection seems largely a concern of men. All of the respondents who mentioned talk of love by the partner as a negative postintercourse experience were male:

Talk about marriage and love. (man, 26)

Expressions of never-ending love. (man, 27)

I would feel horrible if my partner expressed love, or hung out for long periods or hassled me about things that were made clear. (man, 30)

Anything too possessive, cute, or cloying. (man, 39)

I would not like her to get up and go away, but not to be overly loving and caressing either. (man, 25)

Love at first sight is very unusual. So, too, is love at first lovemaking, especially where there is a small interval of time between sighting and sex. But women, for reasons that strike us as basically natural and healthy, often develop feelings of affection for their sexual partners more quickly than men, and are far more likely than men to express their feelings quite openly in the postcoital period. We are not suggesting that there is anything wrong with having these feelings, of course, nor are we suggesting that the feelings not be expressed. What we are saying, based on the results of our study, is that the *timing* of this expression is important. Yes, the feelings of sexual excitement and orgasm and afterplay are interpretable, and often rightly so, as affection, even as love. But your partner may not be feeling the same way you do, if it is early in the relationship. Saying something like, "I love you" or "I want to live with you forever" right after your first or second sexual encounter may well break your partner's positive mood. If you feel loving, you can let your partner know—but at another time. You will be in more control, and you will be more certain of your feelings toward your partner.

In movies the partners may reach simultaneous orgasm the first time they have sex, and then reveal their undying love for each other at exactly the same postorgasmic moment. In life, things usually move along more slowly—and unevenly. You may be eager to hear loving words before your partner is. All we are suggesting is that there are times in the early stages of a relationship when you should pause before saying things your partner may not be ready to hear.

Some people—mostly men—may seem never to be ready. They feel uncomfortable when partners with whom they have been living for years express love. They may, in fact, deeply love their partners, yet feel uncomfortable verbalizing such strong emotional responses themselves. Words we find hard to say ourselves may trouble us when others say them. On the other hand, when we *can* say something extravagant, hearing it from another becomes less discomforting and, in the case of love, downright pleasurable. This is why men in this situation stand to gain by trying to let themselves go a little. If things are basically good in your relationship, and you feel really good about your partner, say so after sex. You don't have to begin with, "I am totally and completely wild about you and you mean more to me than anyone ever has." You might simply say, "I feel really good about us" or "I love you."

Mundane and Irrelevant Conversation

It is very difficult to fully enjoy a vacation from work unless you go away. If you stay at home, there always seem to be things that need doing. Bills keep coming in, repairs always have to be done on the house, and people from whom you would rather not hear keep calling. When you are even a hundred miles away, you simply cannot do anything about any of these problems and thus it becomes possible to forget about them—which is what makes your trip a vacation.

As we have said, intercourse and orgasm at home can be a mini-vacation. Although you are physically home, your mind can be occupied with the pleasures of intimacy. Many components of our respondents' ideal afterplay had the quality of a romantic vacation about them: a peaceful atmosphere, sensual foods and cool drinks, soft lights and music. It is no wonder then that many people—both men and women—told us they did not like discussions of responsibilities, problems, and so on during the postintercourse period. A wide variety of topics and conversational directions were mentioned:

Talking about inane things or bringing up responsibilities that we have to meet are objectionable to me. (man, 34)

Making plans for the day. (woman, 26)

Talk about business or professional matters. (man, 35)

Talk about house and financial problems. (man, 39)

I would not want a discussion that would require decision-making. (man, 26)

I don't like him to say things totally unrelated to what we've just done after we're through. Sometimes he does this, e.g., "I've got to play basketball at 7:30 tomorrow." (woman, 20)

Discussions about bills or taxes. Melodramatic seriousness. A sudden return of worries about work, etc. (man, 37)

I do not want to talk of problems or purely practical, mundane matters. If, for instance, he jumped out of bed, gave me several directions for errands I had to run, laid out plans for the weekend, and expressed his concern over his aging parents, I would be either livid or depressed for hours. (woman, 40)

The last quote shows two of the more serious consequences of allowing your postcoital conversation to drift in the direction of everyday worries and concerns: depression and anger. We all know how quickly even thinking about problems with work, money, or relatives can make us unhappy. When these subjects are discussed, the potential for unhappiness remains and is joined by the possibility of a fight.

Some topics may be inadvisable for your afterplay though perfectly all right for someone else's. In fact, what may be a topic you should keep away from now could, at some other time in your life together, be a good subject for postcoital conversation. Perhaps the best example of this, because it is so important a topic, is *children.*

Some people mentioned discussion of their children as part of ideal afterplay; others described it as a negative postintercourse experience. Those who said that they didn't like to talk about their children after sex did not go into details, but there are a number of possible reasons. For example, the two parents may be in disagreement about some aspect of dealing with the child. Or it may be simply one of those times (labeled as "a phase") when almost every child will try the parents' patience, when neither parent has the slightest idea as to how to deal with the child.

Even if your discussions do not drift into areas of disagreement, simply talking about "mundane" topics (this adjective was used by a number of respondents) is destructive of good afterplay, especially within the first few minutes. The romantic, intimate mood of good afterplay is both more fleeting and more fragile than the "mood for sex." As such, protective care must be taken lest we end it too soon.

A 25-year-old professional woman mentioned three other categories of conversation that could end the romantic mood for many of us: "Bringing up something irrelevant that happened that day. Talking about other people. Talking about what's going to happen tomorrow."

Discussion of Sex and Performance

He: "How was I?"
She: "You *were* terrific."

How many men have prevented, damaged, or ruined a relationship by asking their partner directly after sex whether or not she had an orgasm, either in the thinly veiled way cited above (another equally subtle variant is "How was it for you?") or the very direct "Did you come?"

This inquiry, which may be selfish as well as or rather than solicitous, is the most familiar example of a type of conversation many people said they did not like after sex—what a 31-year-old woman called "an analysis of the act itself." Many members of both sexes do not enjoy this:

I would not like undue discussions of the sex act itself (i.e., a play-by-play account). This would sort of ruin what happened. (man, 24)

I really hate it when a man starts to analyze every move that's been made during intercourse. (woman, 40)

Analysis of our lovemaking. (man, 35)

I don't like egotistical comments about performance. (woman, 22)

In-depth analysis of the sex that has just occurred. I'd not want her analyzing it, or us. (man, 37)

Complain about or discuss sexual preferences, i.e., I didn't like that. (man, 35)

I don't like to talk about all the intricate details of my sexual experiences, i.e., how often my tremors came, why I didn't reach orgasm. I don't like to talk in clinical or psychological terms about the intercourse prior. (woman, 21)

Note how often the word "analyze" is used in the above descriptions. A glance at the dictionary definition of this word makes it clear why many people dislike postcoital analysis: "Analyze—to separate into constituent parts; determine the elements of; to examine critically, so as to give the essence of." *Lovemaking does not end with orgasm!* But to analyze, to separate into parts, even to be critical (we have already seen the problems of criticism in afterplay) is likely to make us feel that it *has* ended. And that it was not so absorbing an experience, either.

Suppose for a moment that you and a friend have just seen a movie. You absolutely loved it, and became totally immersed in it. Even now, a few minutes later, you are still not back on earth. Suddenly, your friend begins an analytical discussion of what you have shared (or thought you had shared). Even if his or her comments are basically positive, your experience has been spoiled. You would not mind talking about the movie at another time, but not right now.

Not right now. This is an important phrase when afterplay is involved.

We are not suggesting that you and your partner should never discuss your sexual likes and dislikes. In fact, we agree with most contemporary writers on sexuality who consider such discussions to be a healthy, perhaps even necessary, component of a good relationship. But the period after sex is a time to be enjoyed for its own pleasures.

Andy L. is a young man on the verge of experiencing fully such pleasures. But he is overly concerned with performance, and occasionally lets postcoital conversation drift in directions that could diminish his and his partner's enjoyment.

Things that bother us

Andy L. is an instructor at a state university in the southwest. About a month ago he met Fran, a student, and they have been seeing each other just about every night since. He is 26, she is 22. Andy says that he is content with all aspects of this relationship. He is also pleased with their frequency of sexual relations, which is four to six times a week.

He believes that he is fully satisfying his current partner, but some previous partners have not reached orgasm with him. What he does at such times "depends on frequency of occurrence. If it occurs during the early stages of formation of a relationship, I usually feel that dysfunction is due to novelty and/or anxiety, attempt to console my partner, and don't give it another thought. If my partner wants to discuss it, I try to find the source of the problem. After several weeks together, if the problem persists, I either look for problems in the relationship or feel that my partner and I are not right for each other."

Of his afterplay, Andy says, "I'm extremely satisfied with my current after-coitus experience. I especially enjoy being close, both physically and mentally. Knowing that my partner has been satisfied and is happy gives me a tremendous amount of pleasure." What is this afterplay? "I hug and caress my partner and engage in some conversation; telling my partner how good I feel when close to her. Other topics range from events in our daily lives to things that bother us about one another." Andy omitted the response to our question, "How often do you praise your partner?" objecting to the word "praise": "I don't 'praise' my partner since I feel this involves a comparison to previous partners and, as such, is inappropriate and insensitive. I will comment that I feel very satisfied with my partner. (With this interpretation in mind, my answer to this question would be 'almost always.')"

What kind of postcoital experience would be disagreeable for him? "An unsatisfied partner who is frustrated and jumps out of bed (to get away from me). I don't think any derogatory comments from her would make me feel any worse than my own feelings of failure (shortcomings?)."

For many women the most offensive kind of postcoital analysis is the question mentioned at the start of this section—"Did you come?" or its equivalent (many comments that men make are simply more delicate ways of saying the same thing—"How was it for you?" "Are you OK?" "Well?" "Did you . . .?" and so on). In her article, "Orgasm: Pleasure or Tyranny?" Judith Coburn writes, "The questions 'Are you OK?' or the more direct 'Did you come?' can be two of the most unwelcome in the English language. As female orgasm has become the new measure of sexual success, those questions are asked with increasing frequency these days." [5] We cannot be certain that the frequency has increased recently—although this seems likely—but based on what our respondents told us, the question is still a common one, and it is for many women unwelcome:

I don't want to talk about the fact that I didn't have an orgasm. (woman, 27)

Asks if he were any good. (woman, 24)

I don't like anyone to ask me if I came—'cause I often don't with normal intercourse. (woman, 24)

I would not like my partner to ask me: Did you come? How many times? (woman, 25)

Did you come? (particularly when it is not in the context of offering to pleasure me to orgasm if I should want or need it). (woman, 34)

The last quote hints at one reason women do not like to be asked about orgasm—the question, while it seems a sign of concern for *her*, may more often be a sign of *self*-concern. This and other reasons were spelled out by a 31-year-old woman whom we interviewed:

After intercourse, I don't like to be asked if I had an orgasm. If I did have one, it annoys me that my partner had no sense of it. If I didn't come, I'm sometimes disappointed and don't like to have to report on it.

In any case being asked about climaxing is like an interrogation. It's up to me to comment on it or not. I don't want to be put on the witness stand. Anyway, that question from a man always seems, in reality, to translate, "Wasn't I great?"

These comments come, incidentally, from a highly orgasmic woman, one who experiences orgasm about 80 percent of the time and often three or four times during a session of lovemaking. In fact, our study indicates that highly orgasmic women are at least as, if not more bothered by the "did you come" query as are those for whom orgasm is rare.

Some men, whose orgasm rates are nearly 100 percent, have

had the experience of being asked if they came. One man told us that his partner said shortly after his orgasm, "You didn't come, did you?" He was quite upset by the question, especially given its phrasing, mainly because he could not believe that his partner did not even notice what was so overwhelming to him. Men who are in the habit of asking women this question, regardless of how they phrase it, should think for a moment how they would feel if, after orgasm, they were asked, "Did you come?" And, men, imagine how you would feel if you had yet to reach orgasm and were asked by a woman who herself was obviously "finished," "Well, how was I?"

We could not improve on the words of a 26-year-old woman, who has sex often and reaches orgasm nearly two-thirds of the time: "I intensely dislike being asked, 'Did you have an orgasm,'" she wrote. "If it's not obvious let it go—unless I volunteer that information." This is excellent advice for both sexes.

If a woman who did not have an orgasm is asked if she did, she is placed in a difficult position. She can answer truthfully, which might lead to an unpleasant or uncomfortable discussion punctuated with analysis or apologies; or she can decrease the likelihood of honest and intimate communication in the postcoital period by saying she did have one. If you are genuinely concerned about whether or not your partner is sexually satisfied and she does not volunteer the information, you can always ask about it *later*.

Telling and Faking

A major difference between the male and female orgasm is, of course, the phenomenon of ejaculation, which leaves physical proof that orgasm has occurred. Although retarded ejaculation can sometimes occur (it is the male equivalent of the woman who reaches high levels of arousal but finds orgasm difficult to attain), the man has little recourse—it is far more difficult for him to fake it.

In the woman, the physical signs of orgasm are less visible, more transient, although they do exist. For most men, it is the woman's breathing rate, and sounds, that make him believe she is experiencing orgasm. And the term "make him believe" is apt. A woman can fake orgasms, and, according to Hite, and many other authors, most women have done so at least on occasion and many do so regularly. Women's feelings about faking seem to have changed markedly in the last ten years. In *The Sensuous Woman,* author "J" wholeheartedly and unabashedly urged women to fake orgasm, claiming that by so doing they might even bring real orgasms on.[6]

Today, however, feelings are mixed. According to Hite, many women who used to fake orgasms no longer do so. Hite seems to approve of this change, though she does not say so directly. Coburn directly addresses the controversy when she writes, "To women who refuse to fake it, women who do are the enemy—giving men false expectations about female sexuality. Faking it is to most men and many women a basic violation of the intimacy and trust the best lovemaking entails."[7] Furthermore, a basically orgasmic woman who fakes it when she doesn't come is damaging her partner's chances of making sex better for her—he can't be expected to please her more if he thinks he already is. Often what's involved is a minor matter of timing.

As we see it, the whole issue of faking and telling will be moot when men and women both realize that the sexual encounter involves much more than orgasm.

When people experience difficulties in sex, the kind that bring them to a therapist—whether it is a man experiencing erectile problems or a woman who is not reaching orgasm—the "treatment," nondemand pleasuring, consists of the partners giving each other physical pleasure without trying to achieve erections or orgasms. It is a remarkably simple approach, and it is remarkably successful. We see no reason why you have to wait to have problems before instituting nondemand pleasuring. If you and your partner can agree that neither of you will demand anything of the other in sex, your sex is almost bound to improve. When nothing is demanded, nothing has to be faked.

We have spent a great deal of time on discussions of performance for two reasons. First, it is a behavior in which many people engage, unaware that it is not particularly good for developing or sustaining a relationship and may, in fact, be quite detrimental. Second, classification of "performance discussions" as negative by many people, and as ideal by practically no one, corroborates the prevailing view in the field of human sexuality today: Most of our sexual problems are due to excessive concern with sex as performance, and to the "performance anxiety" which may ensue.

Often it is only during afterplay that performance concerns are expressed. Those who worry that their partners will grill them, or criticize them, or analyze their every move, would probably be happy to see them disappear as soon as the postintercourse period begins. The best way to avoid this is to stop thinking of sex as a performance and start thinking of it as a way to feel good and close to someone else. When the sex happens to be really satisfying physically, that's an added benefit. If you are in a basically sound relationship, what your partner really wants is *you*, not a machine.

As Ingrid Bengis has written in *Combat in the Erogenous Zone*:

> A little awkwardness can be far more personal than a lot of polish. Spectacular showmanship, while it can leave you breathless with excitement, seems like a sadly empty performance arena once the tents have folded. As for "skills," no woman wants a technocrat in bed next to her; she wants a human being like herself.[8]

Praise of "Sexual Performance"

I don't like to be praised for my sexuality—I'd like to know what my partner feels about me. (woman, 27)

The film *An Unmarried Woman* examines with great sensitivity the plight of a woman whose husband leaves her for another. At first, as is often the case, she is uneager to meet men and resists sexual advances. However, on the advice of a psychologist, a woman, she allows herself to say yes to a man she knows from work. Although his initial foreplay leaves something to be desired, the sex—what we see of it—seems good. In fact, for him at least it is terrific. Shortly after, he expresses his satisfaction by telling her, essentially, that her husband was a fool for leaving such a good thing. Superficially, this would seem to be an ego-boost for her, but she leaves unhappy and angry. She does not see him again.

How can it be that praise is ever unwelcome? A large number of people described hearing compliments about themselves and their lovemaking as ideal afterplay. Also, as we shall see later, our statistical analysis revealed a positive correlation between how often a person is praised after sex and how satisfied he or she is with the postintercourse experience. But there are different kinds of praise—there is praise of the sex itself and praise of the person. It is the latter that people find highly reinforcing; the former, while it can be pleasant, even exciting, can sometimes be poor afterplay.

There are several variables determining whether praise is harmful or helpful. First, there may be a sex difference. Fewer men than women said they disliked praise of their sexual behavior. Second, praise often derives its value from its context. For example, praise may be fine if it is combined with genuine statements of affection. But when the praise is crude—as in Mary Gordon's *Final Payments,* in which a man starts the postintercourse period with "You got a great future ahead of you, honey, the way you need it and those terrific tits"[9]—it can hurt. Third, there is the quality and nature of the relationship. If yours is a stable one, each of you relatively certain of the other's commitment, positive comments about the sex itself can enhance afterplay. Again we find that as soon as sex is looked upon as a performance (even an applauded one) *separated from the person,* the afterplay and hence the entire sexual encounter may be spoiled. This is most likely to happen when the praise is in the form of a comparison or is perceived as a comparison to other partners, current or previous.

I do not wish to have the act performed, praised or compared to other women or experiences. (woman, 21)

If my partner would comment on how "good" I was physically without following with an "I love you" or at least physically showing tender affections toward me, I'd feel I was being rated—a definitely negative experience. (woman, 27)

Talk About Other Partners (Comparisons)

Although many men directly ask for a comparison when they ask "How was I?," more and more of them are finding that, like women, they are not interested in being compared with other sexual partners. Several men specifically mentioned the fact that they would not like such comparisons (e.g., "talk about other men") in afterplay. But again it is women who find such comparisons particularly unpleasant—perhaps because they, more often than men, have experienced them:

I do not like any reference to past experiences with other partners. (woman, 25)

I also do not consider comparing the sexual experience with me to that which my partner had had previously with someone else a pleasant experience. (woman, 33)

Compare sexual performance with that of a previous partner. (woman, 32)

Comparing me to another lover. Or fantasy of another. (woman, 28)

I don't like to talk about the tomorrows or other women. (woman, 32)

Can't stand comparison to other partners. (woman, 27)

This rejection of comparison extends even to favorable ones. A 25-year-old woman stated the matter beautifully when she wrote, "I would not like to hear comments about how the relations he has with me might compare to those he might have with others *(even if favorably)* at that time. It might be a topic for discussion at another point, but *not immediately after intercourse.*" (The italics are ours.) Again we see the sensitive nature of the postintercourse period. This woman would not mind so much hearing *some other time* that she rates high sexually. But to hear it immediately is to imply that, for her partner, it is over.

Obviously some things are always unpleasant to hear, and any unpleasantness tends to be magnified in the vulnerable postorgasmic period. But others things are said in afterplay which seem to be unique to this period, and are decidedly negative. Queries such as "How was I?," "Did ya come?," analysis of the sex act, comparisons, and sometimes even praise all mean evaluations of something that has ended. The moment you begin to get involved in such evaluations, the lovemaking is already in the past; the intimacy has ended and so have the good feelings.

CHAPTER 7

The Four Phases

Psychologists have the peculiar distinction of being examples of what they study (a situation not found, for instance, among botanists). Psychologists are also in the extraordinary habit of discussing human beings—their thoughts, their feelings, their actions—as numbers. But if their interest in statistics sometimes seems dehumanizing, its effects are generally salutary. Although personal observations are most often valuable, sometimes "seeing with your own eyes" actually disguises and distorts the truth. If, for example, you were to meet a homosexual who was unstable and unable to work well, you might conclude that homosexuals are unstable and unable to work well. But if you were to see statistical proof (as you could find it in *Homosexualities* by Alan Bell and Martin Weinberg) that the vast majority of homosexuals are as stable and competent as heterosexuals,[1] you would have a much more realistic conception. Kinsey's two landmark volumes were filled with numbers. It was these numbers as much as what Kinsey had to say about them that revolutionized American views on sexuality.

In this chapter, we present data. Our numbers will be based on responses to the short-answer questions, but we will from time to time offer a quote from a respondent to serve as a reminder that these numbers are not about cars, or money, or heights of mountains; they are about people. (If you have not tried the questionnaire yourself, you might do so now. It appears in Chapter 2.)

The Phases

Both physically and psychologically, a sexual encounter can be divided into four phases, all of which or any one of which can occur: foreplay, intercourse, orgasm, and afterplay. These are similar to the four phases of the sexual response cycle described by Masters and Johnson in *Human Sexual Response* (1966) and discussed in texts on human sexuality published since then. However, the similarity (aside from orgasm) is a rough one. Masters and Johnson's phases—excitement, plateau, orgasm, and resolution—are defined in terms of anatomical and physiological changes, many of which are difficult or impossible to observe outside of the laboratory.[2] For example, a woman cannot see her uterus elevate as she progresses from the excitement to the plateau phase, and a man is unlikely to notice the color of his penis change as he moves from early excitement toward orgasm.

The four phases we propose are self-evident. A person may not know when he has moved from the excitement to the plateau phase, but everyone knows when foreplay stops and intercourse begins. If our questionnaire had asked people to describe how long they remained, say, in the plateau phase, we are certain they would have had a great deal more trouble in answering. Unless otherwise specified, any reference we make to phases will be to the easily recognizable sequence of foreplay, intercourse, orgasm, and afterplay.

Many of the items in the questionnaire asked directly about these phases—especially, of course, the last. Two items actually made explicit reference to all of them (although we used the word "period" rather than phase): Question 34 asked how important each of the phases was to the respondent; Question 35 asked how important the respondent thought each phase was for his or her partner. The questions invited the respondent to rate importance on a scale of 1 to 5, 1 meaning "totally unimportant" and 5 meaning "very important."

Since we asked people to tell us how important they believed each phase was to their partner, we were able to see the extent to which men and women were accurate in perceiving the reactions of their opposite sex partners (the great majority of respondents were heterosexual).

The average importance ratings for men, and the *perception* of these ratings by women were as follows:

Phase	Men's self-ratings	Women's ratings of importance to men
Foreplay	4.44	3.99
Intercourse	4.41	4.52
Orgasm	4.50	4.62
Afterplay: first five minutes	3.62	3.54

Obviously, none of the phases is considered unimportant by men, but there is a rather substantial drop from orgasm to afterplay. We have not nor will we strictly assign a duration for afterplay, but our data suggest that the first 15 to 20 minutes after intercourse are especially important. Interviews and responses to other questions indicate that the reported importance of afterplay is highest in the minutes following intercourse and diminishes over time. Women's perceptions of how the men feel is fairly accurate—except for foreplay, where they underestimate its importance to men.

For women (and how they are perceived by men) the situation is rather different:

Phase	Women's self-ratings	Men's ratings of importance to women
Foreplay	4.51	4.38
Intercourse	4.28	4.31
Orgasm	3.98	4.34
Afterplay: first five minutes	4.10	3.84

On the average, women consider the first five minutes of afterplay slightly more important than orgasm (although for women as well as men foreplay is important). Men's perceptions are least accurate with respect to orgasm and the first five minutes of afterplay. They overestimate the importance of orgasm for women and underestimate the importance of afterplay. This is understandable. Recent books and articles on sexuality have paid a tremendous amount of attention to the woman's orgasm and the ways a man can help her achieve it. They have paid essentially no attention to afterplay.

But asking a person directly how important something is to him or her is only one way—and probably not the best way—to measure importance. Direct verbal reports are sometimes misleading. Social psychologists have found that there is not always a close correspondence between what people say is important to them and what actually is important. Psychologist Harold Kelley asked people how important hearsay was in determining first impressions. His respondents said it was unimportant. Yet when this was tested experimentally, the findings revealed that hearsay is very important in determining such impressions.[3]

Also, we may often underestimate the importance of things because we take them for granted. For example, the full importance of a relationship may not be appreciated until it is threatened; the value and importance of a job may not be realized until it is lost. Scientists sometimes get a more accurate idea of how important something is by a somewhat less direct manner than asking about it point blank. And so we learned, using an indirect approach, that afterplay is far more important to men and women than they say it is. We learned this by using correlations—a statistic.

Importance and Correlation

When we say something is important, we mean that it matters, that it makes a difference. One of the chief tasks of psychological research is to discover what does and does not matter to psychological health. Does it matter, for example, how you were toilet trained, or what color the walls are in your kitchen, or what you do after intercourse? Are any of these aspects of our lives related to psychological well-being?

One way to find answers to these questions is to look at correlations. For example, if you know the toilet-training experiences of a hundred individuals and then get some measure of their mental health, you can easily see whether or not there is any correlation between the two. In certain cases, correlations are obviously present. For example, there is a clear correlation between adult height and weight: Taller adults tend to weigh more than shorter ones.

r

Psychology has a very convenient and easy to understand measure of how closely two variables are related. It is called Pearson's correlation coefficient, and it is generally abbreviated to one letter, *r*. This statistic is widely used in the social sciences and is described in virtually every introductory statistics text. We recognize that some readers are fearful of statistics and numbers, but an understanding of correlation is useful for a full understanding of our findings. To know that 22 percent of our sample spend 20 minutes or more in physical contact after intercourse is interesting. But to know—as we found—that the longer you spend in physical contact after sex, the more you are satisfied with your relationship, is not only interesting but helpful.

The value of *r* is a direct reflection of the direction of the relationship between two variables and the strength of this relationship. When *r* is positive, it means that high values of one variable generally mean high values of the other—adult height and weight is a good example. A negative *r* means the relationship is of the opposite type: An example is age and the number of hairs on the head, especially for men. Whereas more inches of height typically mean more pounds of weight, more years (sad to say) tend to mean *fewer* hairs. When *r* is zero, or close to zero, it means that the two variables are essentially unrelated. An example of this—from our data—is the correlation between age and satisfaction with foreplay, which was +.10 for men and −.06 for women.

r can go from −1.00 to +1.00, either of which means a perfect correlation. When *r* is 1.00 (plus or minus) it means exact prediction is possible. Such correlations are nonexistent in psychology, and rare even in the physical sciences.

Another way to think of *r* is as a measure of predictability: knowing an adult's height, we can make a fairly good prediction of his or her weight; knowing a man's age permits us to make a reasonably good guess about his hair.

Between 0 and 1 (or 0 and −1) the value of *r* is a shorthand measure of the strength of the association between two variables. The greater the value of *r*, the stronger the correlation. The following table should help you interpret the data we will present (some of our examples are from baseball, a statistics-conscious sport).

0 to .19:   no correlation, or a correlation so small as to be insignificant.

.20 to .39:   substantial correlation. The correlation between the IQs of parents and their adopted children is .28. The correlation between lifetime batting average and total home runs is about .35.

.40 to .59:   strong correlation. For growing children, the correlation between age and height is about .50. The correlation between lifetime batting average and total RBIs is about .47.

.60 and above: very strong correlation. The r for adult height and weight is about .70.

What is most important for our purposes is that the larger the value of r, the greater the correlation.

Now let's take a look at the correlations between satisfaction with the four phases of the sexual encounter and overall satisfaction with the relationship. In doing so we can see how *each* of the four phases is connected or associated with overall satisfaction, which helps us more accurately determine the importance of each of the phases. How much do each of the four phases matter? To what extent does each make a difference? We were most curious, of course, about the fourth phase.

Sex and Satisfaction

If we had to choose the most important item in our questionnaire it would probably be Question 38, How satisfied are you with your overall relationship with your partner? Most of the people in our sample seem to be satisfied with their relationships. The exact percentages were:

	Percentages	
Response	Men	Women
Very satisfied	38.7	42.9
Satisfied	35.5	26.4
Somewhat satisfied	15.1	15.7
Somewhat dissatisfied	9.7	8.6
Dissatisfied	1.1	3.6
Very dissatisfied	0	2.9

There is variability in our sample; not everyone is happy. To the extent that the sexual experience contributes to overall satisfaction, how much do the four phases contribute? If, as we and many others strongly believe, the sexual life of a couple is one of the major components of what we call a "good relationship," what aspects of sex are most important?

Foreplay

Question 16 asked "To what extent are you satisfied with your typical foreplay experience?" Reponses were:

	Percentages	
Response	Men	Women
Very satisfied	32.3	37.6
Satisfied	48.4	41.1
Somewhat satisfied	15.1	12.8
Somewhat dissatisfied	3.2	3.5
Dissatisfied	1.1	3.5
Very dissatisfied	0	1.4

What is the correlation between satisfaction with foreplay and satisfaction with the overall relationship? In order to compute r one needs numbers, so we assigned a 1 to Very satisfied, a 2 to Satisfied, and so on to a 6 for Very dissatisfied. r was .59 for men and .24 for women. Stated simply, this means that there is quite a close association between a man's satisfaction with foreplay and how he perceives the condition of his whole relationship. This is consistent with his ratings of importance (response to Question 34) discussed earlier. For women, however, the correlation—while it exists—is not so strong. This does not mean that foreplay is unimportant to women, but it does indicate that it may not be quite so important as the responses to Question 34 imply. You may recall that when we asked *directly*, women named foreplay as the most important of all the phases.

We were also interested in knowing how much time people spend in foreplay. Here are the responses to Question 14, "How much time do you and your partner typically spend in foreplay behavior?"

	Percentages	
Response	Men	Women
Less than five minutes	5.4	5.7
Five to fifteen minutes	44.1	44.7
Fifteen to thirty minutes	40.9	31.2
Thirty minutes or more	9.7	18.4

Are people happy with the amount of time they spend in foreplay? Question 15 asked how much time people would *like* to spend relative to the time they actually spend. Responses were:

	Percentages	
Response	Men	Women
Much more	7.6	7.1
Somewhat more	28.3	31.7
The same	62.0	59.7
Somewhat less	2.2	1.4
Much less	0	0

This is pleasant data. The percentage profiles for the two sexes are nearly identical, and the vast majority of people are either content with the amount of time they spend or would like to spend just a little more time.

Intercourse

Although the concept of afterplay can be extended to include the period following any sexual activity, it generally refers to the post*intercourse* period. Thus sexual intercourse is central to the definition of afterplay. As you will recall from the earlier discussion, intercourse was rated as highly important for both sexes and each had a realistic perception of its importance for the opposite sex. It is not surprising, then, that most of the people in our sample reported high levels of satisfaction with their intercourse experience. Question 21 asked "How satisfied are you with your experience during actual intercourse?" The answers were:

	Percentages	
Response	Men	Women
Very satisfied	53.8	44.3
Satisfied	37.6	35.7

	Percentages	
Response	Men	Women
Somewhat satisfied	6.5	7.9
Somewhat dissatisfied	1.1	8.6
Dissatisfied	1.1	2.1
Very dissatisfied	0	1.4

Again satisfaction levels are high, especially for men, over 90 percent of whom are satisfied or very satisfied with intercourse.

How often did our respondents engage in this generally satisfying activity? In Question 17 we asked, "Approximately how many times per week do you and your partner engage in sex?"

The average was twice a week, broken down as follows:

	Percentages	
Response	Men	Women
Less than once a week	18.3	14.9
Once a week	14.0	19.1
2–3 times a week	39.8	39.7
4–6 times a week	19.4	19.1
More than six times a week	8.6	7.1

More than half of each group wanted to have sex more often— the exact percentages are 65 percent of the men and 60 percent of the women (only 3 percent wanted to have sex less often). If men and women both feel this way, why don't they simply have intercourse more often?

Of course it is not that easy, as nearly everyone who has ever tried to leave more time for play has found out. Children play. Adults *have* children, adults work, and they develop habits.

How can these habits be changed? Perhaps part of the answer

lies in the variables that are associated with frequency. Our statistics show that for men there are not many such variables, and only two that a woman can easily do something about: Compliments and romantic conversation after intercourse. The man who often hears both at that time will have intercourse more often than the man who does not. For the woman there are many variables associated with how often she will have sex. But the male behaviors most closely associated with the woman's interest—as shown by frequency—are holding her and talking romantically *afterward.*

Most people would like to have intercourse more often. These statistics tell us that what happens after sex is clearly related to how often we engage in it.

Orgasm

Orgasm has been described as "the summit of physical and emotional gratification in sexual activity," and most first-person accounts of this "highly pleasurable, tension-relieving, seizure-like response" [4] show that there is no need to ask people whether or not they are satisfied with the experience of orgasm. Orgasm is a subject of great controversy today, but about one of its aspects there is no dispute: It feels extremely good.

For reasons which are unclear—the general view being that they are primarily social and psychological in origin—men are more likely to experience orgasm in a sexual encounter than women. Our data simply confirm this. In Question 19 we asked, "Approximately what percentage of the times you have sex do you reach orgasm?" The responses were:

	Percentages	
Response	Men	*Women*
0–9% of the time	0	7.2
10–19%	0	3.6
20–29%	0	2.2

Response	Percentages	
	Men	Women
30–39%	0	3.6
40–49%	0	3.6
50–59%	0	7.2
60–69%	0	6.5
70–79%	2.2	12.2
80–89%	3.2	9.4
90–100% of the time	94.6	44.6

Although, on the average, a woman is less likely to achieve orgasm, when she does she is more likely than the man to have more than one. There is nothing in males to match the phenomenon of "multiple orgasm" in females. A man may have more than one orgasm in a session, and may even be able to achieve several during intercourse prior to the ejaculatory one, but the experience of having successive orgasms which gain in intensity is an experience foreign to virtually all men.

Question 20 asked, "How many orgasms do you have during a typical lovemaking session?"

Response	Percentages	
	Men	Women
0	0	7.9
1	76.3	51.8
2	17.2	27.3
3	4.3	7.9
4	2.2	2.9
5	0	0
6	0	1.4
7	0	0.7

Whereas less than a quarter of the men we sampled said they typically had more than one orgasm in a sexual encounter, 40 percent of the women said they did.

With respect to both consistency of orgasmic response (as measured by Question 19 on percentages) and within-session frequency (Question 20), women are far more variable than men. Since the vast majority of men experience an orgasm every time or nearly every time they have intercourse, and most have a single one, women are not likely to gauge their adequacy as lovers by their partner's achievement of orgasm. The need to feel that men's sexual excitement and orgasmic response are more than mere reflexes is possibly best reflected by the woman who told us that she liked to feel her husband's penis occasionally become soft in her vagina because she enjoyed so much bringing him to erection again.

The story is altogether different when it comes to the man's perceptions. Since he knows that orgasm for many women has a somewhat elusive quality and that when orgasm is attained it can occur again quickly, he is more likely to judge himself and his sexual technique by his partner's orgasmic response. Perhaps this is why many men spoil the afterplay experience by asking the kinds of questions we discussed earlier. *Our* questions are: To what extent does the woman's orgasm relate to her satisfaction with the relationship? Are the man's concerns about his partner's achieving several orgasms every time they make love justified? Is the female orgasm the secret to a good sexual relationship?

The importance ratings cited earlier suggest a "no" answer to these questions, but were the women in our sample simply *saying* that orgasm is less important to them than foreplay, intercourse, and afterplay? Once again, we looked at a correlation. Did percentage of time orgasm is reached, and number of orgasms reached per session, correlate with satisfaction in the overall relationship? Hardly. For percentage, the r was .19 and for number it was .10. These numbers tell us that there is *no major relationship between the number or the percentage of times orgasm is reached and satisfaction.*

This is not to say that orgasms are unimportant for women.

The majority of women in our sample did achieve orgasm regularly, and among those who never or rarely achieved it with their partners there were several whose relationships seemed clearly to suffer. Also, the mean importance rating of 3.98 for women is not low—in fact, more than a third of the women gave it a rating of 5—Very important. But our data strongly suggest that a good relationship does not require the woman to reach one or more orgasms every time she makes love. This amounts to statistical confirmation of our thesis that sharing and communication are *more* important than orgasm in a loving sexual encounter. Men and women need not be overly concerned about numbers or percentages of orgasms. If this anxiety were eliminated, afterplay would be less a time of performance evaluation and analysis, and more a time for loving.

It is also true that men's orgasms are not significantly related to satisfaction with the relationship. The correlations between overall satisfaction and the orgasmic variables were .13 for percentage and .05 for number per session for the males in our sample. For example, a 33-year-old male having sex four to six times a week, reaching three to four orgasms each time, said he was dissatisfied with his sexual and overall relationship with his partner (whom he had been seeing for five weeks). He was one of the few people to say he thought the questionnaire was geared more toward married couples or people living together than singles, and was the only respondent who said "it was boring." He used the term "relieved" to describe his feelings after intercourse.

We have noted that men regularly reach orgasm and expect women to do the same. Some women who have more than one orgasm even expect their partners to do the same. One respondent told us of a woman who was consistently multi-orgasmic. "She would have three or four orgasms for each one of mine," he said. "The problem was that she expected the same from me." He added, "If after two orgasms I was tired out, she seemed definitely concerned about me and why I was having such troubles."

What we have discovered is a basic misunderstanding between men and women on the question of orgasm much of
which is due to the very human tendency to assume that others
act, feel, and think as we do. Perhaps because we lack information, or because we are naive, or because we desire the security
and comfort that comes with a familiar world, we tend to see
other people as we see ourselves.[5] Our perceptions are therefore
distortions of the truth. Men who feel dissatisfied and frustrated
if they don't reach orgasm every time assume that women must
feel the same way. And women who are happiest with three or
four orgasms may expect men to be happiest with a similar
number. This kind of projection of our feelings on another can
undermine a relationship—or we can recognize them for what
they are, and stop the misunderstanding at its source.

Afterplay

When we asked about satisfaction with afterplay we did not
use the word but rather the more neutral "postintercourse
period." Since we did not then know what people do at this
time, we did not want to take a chance on biasing responses in
the direction of play or any other physical activity.

How satisfied were our respondents with their typical postintercourse experience? Question 32 asked them directly. The
responses were:

| | Percentages | |
Response	Men	Women
Very satisfied	27.2	34.3
Satisfied	46.7	38.6
Somewhat satisfied	16.3	17.1
Somewhat dissatisfied	8.7	5.7
Dissatisfied	1.1	2.1
Very dissatisfied	0	2.1

Clearly there is a lot of good afterplay going on. About 30 percent of our sample said they were very satisfied with their postintercourse experience. However, when compared to the previous tables, these data also show that people are less satisfied with their afterplay than they are with either foreplay or intercourse. Why is this so? It could be, as we indicated earlier, that more people underestimate the significance of afterplay and thus tend to give it the shortest shrift—the least amount of time and attention.

Finally, does it matter whether or not afterplay is satisfying? Does the quality of afterplay correlate with overall satisfaction? Yes, substantially, for both sexes. For men the correlation was .48 and for women it was .40. The significance of these *r*'s can best be appreciated in the summary table which appears below:

Correlations between *satisfaction* with the *overall relationship* and:

	Men	Women
Satisfaction with foreplay	.59	.24
Satisfaction with intercourse	.38	.24
Percentage of time orgasm occurs	.13	.19
Orgasms "per session"	.05	.10
Satisfaction with afterplay (the postintercourse experience)	.48	.40

Satisfaction with afterplay is *most* highly correlated with a good relationship for women, and is not far behind foreplay for men. In absolute terms the correlation for men (.48) is even higher than it is for women. The postintercourse experience, then, is important to both sexes.

Remember that men, when asked directly about the four

phases, *said* that the least important one was afterplay. Yet now we see that second to foreplay, satisfaction with afterplay is *most* associated with satisfaction in the total relationship. This means that afterplay is considerably more important to men than they realize. The situation is even more striking for women. Although women report that afterplay is more important to them than orgasm, they *say* it is not as important as foreplay and intercourse. Yet when we see the correlation between satisfaction with each of the four phases and total satisfaction, we find that the critical, truly significant phase is afterplay. The importance of afterplay as it relates to overall satisfaction has, in fact, been drastically underestimated by both sexes.

Correlation and Causation

A maxim of experimental psychology is that correlation does not necessarily mean causation. For example, there is a positive correlation between the amount of rain on a given day and the number of people carrying umbrellas, yet we do not say that the umbrellas *cause* the rain. We found that satisfaction with afterplay and overall satisfaction are correlated. How can we be sure that satisfying afterplay leads to a satisfying relationship rather than vice versa? On purely statistical grounds, we can not be certain. But for practical purposes, it does not matter. As we have said, trying all at once to have a satisfying total relationship is unlikely to meet with success, at least not in a short time. Trying simply to have satisfying afterplay is a much less awesome task and, at the least, will enrich your total relationship by some satisfying moments, minutes, or hours.

In our survey, certain factors did not correlate (or barely did) with overall satisfaction with the relationship, nor did they correlate with sexual satisfaction. Considering the assorted misconceptions that continue to abound, it seems worthwhile to point these out: geographical location; age; age of partner; number of children living at home; occupation and partner's occupation; length of relationship; method of contraception typically used; importance of foreplay to self; and perceived importance of orgasm for the partner.

It is reassuring to know that some of those variables which would be impossible or very difficult to change—such as age—are unrelated to sexual and overall satisfaction. Although age may bring about a diminishing of sexual frequency, especially in men, the following case illustrates how little effect age need have on afterplay and on sexual or overall satisfaction.

Loved, alive, vibrant and happy

"Directly after intercourse I continue close contact without disengaging, converse romantically, and continue to caress. I feel satisfied, loved, alive, vibrant, happy, gratified, and respected." These are the words of William B., a 62-year-old carpenter who, for the last year, has been seeing a 45-year-old computer programmer. He sees no other women. Bill is extremely happy with all aspects of his relationship, both sexual and otherwise.

Bill and his partner engage in sex often. Before intercourse there may be more than half an hour of foreplay. Afterward, they lie cuddling and fondling for the same length of time. Occasionally there is sleep for both of them soon after sex, but before sleep there is always affectionate and appreciative conversation. For both, the five minutes after orgasm are more important than orgasm itself.

His actual afterplay is close to his ideal, which he describes as "a continuation of caressing and massaging and continued contact. Our words reflect what we are feeling at the moment."

He has an orgasm every time, but "we both recognize that orgasm is not absolutely necessary during lovemaking." There are, he reports, no sexual difficulties.

What would turn him off? "A negative after-intercourse experience would be a 'Thank God it's over' attitude. I would not like my partner to quickly withdraw and turn away from me and fall, immediately, to sleep without a word."

CHAPTER 8

Keeping the Play in Afterplay

No psychologist that we know of has ever put forth a theory that a basic human need is the need to avoid sex. In order to guarantee species survival, nature made certain that sex feels good. But while sex itself feels good for nearly all of us, there is no such universality in the way we feel afterward. Some of us feel frustrated, some feel lonely, some are exhausted, some filled with energy. Many of us feel relaxed after sex; many have feelings of satisfaction. And, finally, there are some people whose feelings justify the term "lovemaking" for the sex act. They experience warmth and love for their partners, which can sometimes be so intense as to lead to a genuine feeling of transcendence.

Feelings are—and, we hope, always will be—somewhat mysterious. If when we awoke each morning we knew exactly how we would feel each hour of the day, getting up would hardly be worthwhile, however good the feelings. But although we may not know precisely how we will feel with certain people and in certain situations, we can have a pretty good idea. Most important, we may find that we have far more control over our feelings than we think we do. We may, in fact, find that doing certain things makes it more likely that we will feel certain ways.

This is the case with afterplay. In Chapters 3 and 4, we talked about many postintercourse activities and feelings. In Chapter 5, we shared with you the postcoital desires of hundreds of people. We listed many different kinds of activities and atmospheres they said they particularly liked, from conversation to candlelight. Now we ask, which are most important? Will the failure to light a candle lead to divorce?

In order to get some idea of priorities, we looked at correlations between various components of afterplay and reported satisfaction with the experience. The results are very reassuring. The most important aspect of afterplay is not whether or not you watch television, read, or eat. It is whether you touch and talk lovingly.

According to our statistical analysis, the most significant aspects of afterplay for a woman are, in order of importance:
1. Her partner wants to remain close to her.
2. He speaks romantically.
3. The five minutes after sex are important to him.
4. He talks to her.
5. The hour after sex is important to him.
6. He stays close to her for more than a few minutes.

For men they are, also in order of importance:
1. His partner speaks romantically to him.
2. The five minutes after sex are important to her.
3. She stays close to him for more than a few minutes.
4. She praises him.
5. She talks to him.
6. She wants to stay close to him.

These, then, are the most basic elements of good afterplay; and if you are able to experience any of them you should be well on the way to improving yours. We realize that it is difficult for some of us, especially men, to speak romantically, but note that your *wanting* to be physically close is even more important to the woman. We also realize that although some women have always been aware of the importance of afterplay, others have not. If they have trouble with romantic conversation, women may enjoy praising their partner. And for men as well as women, just talking can be good afterplay in itself.

Finally, both lists suggest that simply being aware of the importance of afterplay will make it a happier experience.

Are we saying that if you realize the importance of afterplay, are loving to your partner, stay close to him or her, and speak romantically or just pleasantly, you will be a good afterplayer? Yes, that is exactly what we are saying. We realize that for some people this kind of behavior may be difficult at first, but the rewards are definitely worth the attempt. You might keep in mind the fact that afterplay is the last phase of the sexual encounter, which means the good feelings can last into the next day. This is true for a 32-year-old woman, married for seven years, who wrote:

When my husband and I share good moments after sex, be it hugging each other, laughing together or talking and enjoying a favorite food, I go to sleep feeling good and wake up feeling good. The feeling of well-being that lingers after sex continues on into the next morning. Frequently I wake up feeling relaxed and warm and, at first, not even quite sure what's causing the sensation.

Another special quality about the postintercourse period is that afterplay, more than any other aspect of the sexual encounter, offers wide-ranging possibilities for enjoyment. As can be seen in the case of Evelyn J., as long as you keep in mind the very basic notions of loving and sharing, almost anything you do with your partner can be pleasurable.

Caring shared

Evelyn J. is a 32-year-old teacher, married for 11 years, who for the past 4 has been having an affair with another man, a lawyer who is also married. Although they live apart, Evelyn and her lover are able to spend a fair amount of time together, having intercourse about three times a week. Their sexual relationship is extremely good and Evelyn wishes they were able to make love more often than circumstances currently allow.

Both Evelyn and her lover almost always reach orgasm, but when sexual difficulties do arise, their openness and love for each other allow them to deal easily with them. If either of them has not reached an orgasm, ". . . neither of us even hesitates to ask to pleasure the other or to be pleasured if orgasm is wanted. . . ." This is in marked contrast to Evelyn's husband, who often asks her "Did you come?" but who never offers to bring her to orgasm if she wants him to.

However, it is not in the intercourse itself that the differences between Evelyn's two sexual relationships is the sharpest:

"In eleven years of marriage intercourse was intermittently stupendous and generally satisfying, but the postintercourse relationship generated in me anger and frustration due to my husband's withdrawal physically, verbally, and almost always emotionally. I have found in my love partner how much more fulfilling and important the postintercourse time really is. Our actual sexual relations are physically good (as they often are with my husband), but the anticipation of the next sexual experience is much heightened by knowing that the loving and caring shared after intercourse is what, for me, marked the difference between ok/good sexual relations and deep joy and gratification."

Evelyn really enjoys savoring the intimacy, warmth, and relaxation she experiences after sex with her lover: "I love a slowness of voice and movement for a long time after intercourse, whether it is in lying together in bed preparing for sleep or beginning a day with relaxation." Even if they do not have as much time for afterplay as they would like, they always take the time to touch and talk. "We always both dress (even if one of us is in her/his own home) and plan and talk over coffee or tea, holding, touching, having a cigarette."

They are able to incorporate even the routine of preparing for work into the pleasure of their postcoital period. After spending time still entwined from lovemaking and sharing quiet conversation, they gently reenter the day together. She enjoys the pleasures of a shared shower, quietly making the bed together, and the smell of freshly brewed coffee. The time spent with her lover leaves Evelyn feeling ". . . renewed, stronger, and complete."

Obviously, not every lovemaking session need be so thoroughly fulfilling. There will be times when you will be sleepy, times you will want to watch television, times you will not feel particularly romantic, and times you will be interested in a "quickie." There is nothing wrong with this—afterplay is, after all, play, which means there is nothing you *have* to do. On the other hand, certain behaviors can and should be avoided. Arguing with, criticizing, or immediately ignoring your partner is simply bad afterplay—as is comparing your lover to others. And so, too, for many of us, is discussing or analyzing the preceding phases of the sexual encounter as if they were acts in a performance. The attitude that neither sex nor afterplay is a performance is in itself an effective immunization against most sexual difficulties.

Occasional "Problems"

What should afterplay be like when there is early ejaculation, loss of erection, or lack of orgasm? We have alluded to such occurrences throughout the book and in the case histories. If lovemaking is viewed primarily as a time for sharing and loving as opposed to a contest or a performance, then these occurrences will not loom as problems. Here, of course, we are talking about *occasional* premature ejaculation, lack of orgasm, or loss of erection. If they usually or almost always occur, a different approach is needed (see Masters and Johnson's *Human Sexual Inadequacy*). But if you are like most of us, and they happen to you once in a while, there is no need to include apologies, analyses, resentment, blame, guilt, or recrimination in your afterplay. Lovemaking is a time for love.

Even as there are differences in people's afterplay, so are there a variety of ways that people react to these problem situations. One 25-year-old woman's reaction to her husband's occasional premature ejaculation is an excellent example of what shouldn't be done in such cases. She says, "Couldn't you wait a little longer before orgasm?" She then turns away from him, facing the other way, and refuses to say anything further to him.

Fortunately, other women react quite differently to premature ejaculation. One 47-year-old woman said, "I don't make an issue of it. We just take things in stride and don't overreact. We just show our love by staying close together and kissing."

A 24-year-old woman had a common experience—in her first sexual encounter with a man she had known for some time, he ejaculated within a minute. He said, "It can only get better," and neither of them became upset. "In fact," she told us, "afterwards was very nice—cuddling in bed, talking, and drinking wine." Her overall feeling: she had a very nice time and looked forward to seeing him again.

In *Human Sexual Inadequacy*, Masters and Johnson repeatedly emphasize that "fear of inadequacy" is the major factor which undermines a sexual relationship. That is, concern, anxiety, or fear about attaining an erection or an orgasm make you less likely to attain one.

Many women seem to be recognizing this when they reassure their partners who are having difficulties:

Reassurance is probably the single most important thing I could do in such a situation—I, when that arises, make a special effort to be loving, understanding yet not condescending in my listening and speaking on the matter. I'd hope for (and do, in fact, receive) the same "help." (woman, 26)

Sometimes a massage will help relax the person, sometimes fatigue is the problem and sleep is necessary. Positive reinforcement is a must, criticism is a definite no-no. (woman, 25)

I reassure him, but I really don't need to. When he has difficulties we do something else. Having intercourse is not the most important thing or end. (woman, 24)

If my partner is having difficulties I reassure him that it's nothing to worry about. These things happen to everybody at times. I tell him to relax and remind him that our sexual relationship is terrific and the next time will be wonderful. (woman, 33)

Such an attitude of reassurance can often help a man who is having trouble sustaining an erection or having an orgasm. If he is relaxed, he will be more able to focus on pleasure rather than performance, and thus be more likely to be sexually aroused. As one man in his early 40s told us:

If my erection doesn't stay hard all the time, I would like my partner to reassure me that it's OK. I've been in situations like this, with women who say—and they really seem to mean it—that it's OK, that they don't mind, that I should just relax. It's amazing what that will do in terms of getting me hard again!

Although we have often pointed out the differences between men and women, we have found that the most and least desirable kinds of afterplay are the same for both sexes. It is also true that performance anxiety can interfere with a woman's sexual functioning in the same way that it interferes with a man's. A woman anxious about attaining an orgasm may find that her natural sexual responsiveness may be blocked. If a woman seems to be having trouble reaching an orgasm, some men feel compelled to analyze the "problem," others apologize, and still others show annoyance. Fortunately, many men seem to realize that the best thing to do in this situation is to encourage their partners to relax.

I attempt to be comforting, affectionate. I say something like "Oh, well, never mind, there'll be a next time." (man, 33)

Treat it as "no big deal"—still be loving—not apply pressure to perform—not show disappointment—stay close/warm, but "easily" move into another activity—show in words and action that love, loving, being loved is not only sex. (man, 35)

Nothing. It's better to reassure someone that you understand with a touch or a hold, than to try to tell them anything with words. Try to help them to relax, and if you're enjoying yourself, let them know it. (man, 27)

I try to be understanding and loving. And not make a big issue over nothing. Work at it! (man, 25)

I give her my love and support. (man, 21)

I tell her this is a very common thing. Just try and relax. I try to be very supportive, try to give more foreplay, reassuring and holding. (man, 46)

If my partner is having any difficulty, I ask her if there is anything special she would like. But, most important, I try to let her know that it's just terrific being with her, that she makes me feel so good, and that she is very orgasmic. I might even say, "Really, don't worry about it. I love this. Just relax." If she doesn't come, I still feel so good when I do that I let her know it, hug her, squeeze her, and let her know she is wonderful. (man, 38)

We have said many times that a sexual encounter need not be confined to intercourse and orgasm. As long as you realize that sex involves being together, sharing, talking, touching, and loving, then situations which are thought of as problems automatically become less problematic. Through reassurance and relaxation you are likely to improve sexual functioning, and even when intercourse or orgasm are not a part of the encounter, it can still be fulfilling. A 30-year-old woman eloquently summarized our feelings on the matter when she said:

We are not in a competition. There is nothing to be won or lost— we are just here doing this thing together and sometimes it's one thing and sometimes it's another. Orgasm should not be required because then it becomes a burden instead of a delight. I try to help my partner tune into the sensual nature of the experience (touching, tasting, smelling) and to have him appreciate that from time to time there is a grace in accepting one's own rhythm and not pushing it to be what it's not.

Life Style

People are not made up of random bits and pieces of behaviors and feelings. A warm and loving husband is not likely to be an ogre to his children; a person who dislikes and discriminates against one minority group is likely to have negative attitudes toward many groups of people. Similarly, our attitudes toward afterplay cannot be separated or isolated from the rest of our lives. Much more research needs to be done in this area, but already we have indications (significant correlations) that people who do not think it appropriate to talk to close friends about their troubles, and who are attracted to their partners for only physical reasons, are not likely to be happy in their primary relationships. Good afterplay, as we have seen, has little to do with physical qualities and has a great deal to do with the ability to be open and to reveal ourselves intimately.

We have also found that people who disagree with the statement "When I go somewhere in a car, I like to get there as soon as possible with no stops or rests." tend to be happier in their relationships. Perhaps this means that people have better relationships if they are not obsessed with striving for some goal, always trying to get somewhere as fast as they can—with little appreciation for where they are and what they are doing. The simple truth is that people have happier relationships if they take the time to enjoy themselves and other people—if they can play.

Play

Many psychologists feel that children's play is rehearsal and practice for taking their place in the adult world. According to this theory, it is through play that children learn to use objects and tools, to follow rules, to control themselves, to get along with one another, to familiarize themselves with adult duties, responsibilities, and roles. These explanations, however valid, strike us as missing the "just for the fun of it" and "total absorption" aspects of play. Play should mean more than practice for work; otherwise there would be no reason for adults, who are well-practiced in work, to play.

One reason that the "play is practice for work" theory is so popular may be because adults do not often play and rarely do things "for the fun of it"—which may be why they have difficulty enjoying afterplay. Sex is, or certainly should be, play. The terms for the activities surrounding intercourse on either side—foreplay before and afterplay after—have the word "play" within them, and intercourse could just as well be called "mainplay."

Some clinical psychologists believe that the reason so many marriages break up is because one member of the couple or both have no one to play with. Everything we adults do seems to need some rationale, some functional justification. If we stand on a corner, it is to wait for a bus. If we lie on the beach it is to get a suntan. Why do we have to justify everything we do? Play is something to be engaged in for its own sake—just for the fun of it.

A colleague of ours recently taught a graduate seminar on the Psychology of Play. She asked her students to list the playful activities they had engaged in in the last 48 hours. The students had difficulty with this assignment. A few came up with activities like playing records, but no one listed sex and most did not even think it was appropriate to consider sex as a type of play.

For many people, afterplay is bypassed because of the unhappy fact that adults find it so hard to play and enjoy themselves. But sex and afterplay can indeed be playful, and healthy adults can develop the capacity to be childlike in their relationships. Laughing, tickling, singing, talking gibberish, dreaming and fantasizing are all part of good afterplay. If you inevitably omit afterplay in order to get to sleep, because you have a long day ahead of you, your days—without play—will indeed be long.

Most children have the wonderful ability to turn work into play; taking out the trash can become a safari into a wild jungle. Most adults have the unfortunate penchant for turning play into work. You become obsessed with a golf game or tennis and break a club or racket if you don't break par or the opponent's service. As we have seen, for many adults even sex can become an obligation, a competition or a performance to be evaluated.

If afterplay becomes one more thing you have to worry about, our book has failed. If you appreciate the importance and fun of afterplay but your mate doesn't, don't hit him or her with the book—if you do, you have missed the point. You could *show* your partner the book. You can also show him or her the pleasures of afterplay by talking about what you know your partner enjoys, or by touching in the ways and places you think it will be most appreciated.

A Most Important "Don't"

At the end of a serious book on a serious subject, our final suggestion is: Don't be too serious. If you never laugh during afterplay, then the chances are that you have made of it another "assignment," which is exactly what you shouldn't be doing. You may be hugging and caressing or speaking loving words to each other while soft music is playing. Suddenly, the record gets stuck.

The bubble has burst, but you laugh. There will be other days and other bubbles.

NOTES

CHAPTER 1: *What is Afterplay?*
1. Kinsey et al, 1953, pp. 637–638.
2. Warren, 1977, p. 282.
3. DeMott, 1976.

CHAPTER 3: *What People Do*
1. Pengelley, 1974, pp. 80, 88.
2. Kaplan, 1974, p. 31.
3. Freud, 1924/1952, p. 92.
4. Gordon, 1978, p. 137.
5. Babitz, 1976.
6. Tavris and Sadd, 1978, p. 123.

CHAPTER 4: *How People Feel*
1. Young, 1973, p. 749.
2. James, 1902/1958, pp. 377–378.
3. Coleman, 1964; Coleman, 1976, p. 567.
4. Masters and Johnson, 1970.
5. Hite, 1976, p. 86.
6. Masters and Johnson, 1966, pp. 287, 291.
7. Lief, 1966.
8. Masters and Johnson, 1966, pp. 287, 291.
9. Maslow, 1954, p. 235.
10. James, 1902/1958, p. 298.
11. *Ibid.*
12. *Ibid.*, pp. 292–294.

CHAPTER 5: *What People Like*
1. Allport, 1955.
2. Hall, 1966.
3. Lewin, 1936.
4. Jourard, 1974.
5. Jourard and Lasakow, 1958.

6. Jourard, 1959.
7. Masters and Johnson, 1975.
8. Weiss, 1934.
9. Hardy, 1874/1937.

CHAPTER 6: *What People Don't Like*
1. Gordon, 1978, p. 177.
2. Dyer, 1978.
3. McCary, 1975, pp. 282–283.
4. Bach and Wyden, 1968/1970.
5. Coburn, 1978, p. 229.
6. J, 1969/1971.
7. Coburn, 1978, p. 229.
8. Bengis, 1972, pp. 163–164.
9. Gordon, 1978, p. 137.

CHAPTER 7: *The Four Phases*
1. Bell and Weinberg, 1978.
2. Masters and Johnson, 1966.
3. Kelley, 1950.
4. McCary, 1973, p. 192.
5. Halpern and Goldschmitt, 1976.

BIBLIOGRAPHY

Allport, Gordon. *Becoming.* New Haven: Yale University Press, 1955.

Babitz, Eve. "Breakthru in Boudoir Cuisine Revealed." *Ms.,* November, 1976, pp. 74–75.

Bach, George R., and Wyden, Peter. *The Intimate Enemy: How to Fight Fair in Love and Marriage.* New York: Avon, 1970. (Originally published by William Morrow, 1968.)

Becker, Wesley C. *Parents Are Teachers.* Champaign, Illinois: Research Press, 1971.

Bell, Alan P., and Weinberg, Martin S. *Homosexualities: A Study of Diversity Among Men and Women.* New York: Simon & Schuster, 1978.

Bengis, Ingrid. *Combat in the Erogenous Zone.* New York: Knopf, 1972.

Coburn, Judith. "Orgasm: Pleasure or Tyranny?" *Mademoiselle,* May, 1978, pp. 228–229, 265.

Coleman, J. C. *Abnormal Psychology and Modern Life* (3rd ed.). Chicago: Scott, Foresman and Co., 1964).

———*Abnormal Psychology and Modern Life* (5th ed.). Chicago: Scott, Foresman and Co., 1976.

Comfort, Alex. *The Joy of Sex.* New York: Simon & Schuster, 1972.

DeMott, Benjamin. "After the Sexual Revolution." *The Atlantic,* November, 1976, pp. 71–93.

Dyer, Wayne W. *Pulling Your Own Strings.* New York: Thomas Y. Crowell, 1978.

Freud, Sigmund. *A General Introduction to Psychoanalysis.* New York: Washington Square Press, 1952. (Originally published by Boni and Liveright, 1924.)

———*Civilization and Its Discontents.* New York: W. W. Norton & Company Inc., 1962. (Originally published, 1930.)

Gordon, Mary. *Final Payments.* New York: Random House, 1978.

Hall, Edward. *The Hidden Dimension.* New York: Doubleday & Company, Inc., 1966.

Halpern, James, and Goldschmitt, Marvin. "Attributive Projection: Test of Defensive Hypotheses." *Perceptual and Motor Skills,* 1976, 42, pp. 707–711.

Hardy, Thomas. *Far from the Madding Crowd.* New York: Oxford University Press, 1937. (Originally published, 1874.)

Harlow, Harry F. "The Nature of Love." *American Psychologist,* 1958, 13, pp. 673–685.

Heiman, Julia; LoPiccolo, Leslie; and LoPiccolo, Joseph. *Becoming Orgasmic: A Sexual Growth Program for Women.* Englewood Cliffs, N. J.: Prentice-Hall, 1976.

Hite, Shere. *The Hite Report: A Nationwide Study of Female Sexuality.* New York: Macmillan, 1976.

J. *The Sensuous Woman.* New York: Dell 1971. (Originally published by Lyle Stuart, 1969.)

James, William. *The Varieties of Religious Experience.* New York: The New American Library, 1958. (Originally published in 1902.)

Jourard, Sidney M. "Healthy Personality and Self-Disclosure." *Mental Hygiene,* 1959, 43, pp. 499–507.

———*Healthy Personality: An Approach from the Viewpoint of Humanistic Psychology.* New York: Macmillan, 1974.

Jourard, Sidney M., and Lasakow, P. "Some Factors in Self-Disclosure." *Journal of Abnormal and Social Psychology,* 1958, 56, pp. 91–98.

Kaplan, Helen Singer. *The New Sex Therapy.* New York: Brunner/ Mazel, 1974.

Kelley, Harold. "The Warm-Cold Variable in First Impressions of Persons." *Journal of Personality,* 1950, 18, pp. 431–439.

Kinsey, Alfred C.; Pomeroy, Wardell C.; and Martin, Clyde E. *Sexual Behavior in the Human Male.* Philadelphia: W. B. Saunders, 1948.

Kinsey, Alfred C.; Pomeroy, Wardell B.; Martin, Clyde E.; and Gebhard, Paul H. *Sexual Behavior in the Human Female.* Philadelphia: W. B. Saunders, 1953.

Lewin, Kurt. "Some Social Psychological Differences Between the United States and Germany." *Character and Personality,* 1936, 4, pp. 265–293.

Lief, H. I. Teaching doctors about sex. In *An Analysis of the Human Sexual Response,* edited by R. Brecher and E. Brecher. Boston: Little, Brown, 1966.

M. *The Sensuous Man.* New York: Dell, 1972. (Originally published by Lyle Stuart, 1971.)

McCary, James Leslie. *Human Sexuality: Physiological, Psychological and Sociological Factors.* New York: Van Nostrand, 1973.

————*Freedom and Growth in Marriage.* New York: Hamilton (Wiley), 1975.

Maslow, Abraham H. *Motivation and Personality.* New York: Harper & Row, 1954.

Masters, William H., and Johnson, Virginia E. *Human Sexual Response.* Boston: Little, Brown, 1966.

————*Human Sexual Inadequacy.* Boston: Little, Brown, 1970.

————*The Pleasure Bond.* Boston: Little, Brown, 1975.

Newman, Mildred, and Berkowitz, Bernard. *How to Be Your Own Best Friend.* New York: Random House, 1973.

Nye, Robert D. *Three Views of Man.* Monterey, California: Brooks/ Cole, 1975.

Pengelley, Eric T. *Sex and Human Life.* Reading, Mass.: Addison-Wesley, 1974.

Pietropinto, Anthony, and Simenauer, Jacqueline. *Beyond the Male Myth.* New York: Quadrangle, 1977.

Reuben, David. *Everything You Always Wanted to Know About Sex.* New York: Bantam, 1971. (Originally published by David McKay, 1969.)

Ringer, Robert J. *Looking Out for Number 1.* New York: Fawcett Crest, 1977. (Originally published by L. A. Book Co., 1977.)

Rogers, Carl. *On Becoming a Person.* Boston: Houghton Mifflin Company, 1961.

Skinner, B. F. *Science and Human Behavior.* New York: Macmillan, 1953.

Tavris, Carol and Sadd, Susan. *The Redbook Report on Female Sexuality.* New York: Dell, 1978. (Originally published by Delacorte, 1975.)

Warren, Robert Penn. *A Place to Come to.* New York: Random House, 1977.

Weiss, L. A. Differential variations in the amount of activity of newborn infants under continuous light and sound stimulation. *University of Iowa Stud. Child. Welf.,* 1934, 9, No. 4.

Young, P. T. Feeling and emotion. In B. Wolman (Ed.), *Handbook of General Psychology.* Englewood Cliffs, N. J.: Prentice-Hall, 1973.

INDEX